Called to Dance
A Dance Ministry Guidebook

Called to Dance
A Dance Ministry Guidebook

Paryn A. Wallace

BASAR PUBLISHING

Called to Dance

©Copyright 2015 by Paryn A. Wallace

All Scripture quotations, unless otherwise indicated, are taken from the King James Bible Version.

ISBN: 978-1-942013-76-1

Printed in the United States of America.

Cover and Design: Jackie Moore by JDM Designs
                  Additional consulting by Rakia
                  Reynolds, Vanessa Asowata;
                  Skai Blue Media

Editors: Kay Walcott-Henderson and Nicole Bailey-Williams

Dedications

To God be the Glory! With you ALL things are possible. Thank you for never leaving me or forsaking me, even when I did not feel worthy of your calling. I know that your plans are to prosper me and not harm me, your plan gives me hope and a future (Jeremiah 29:11). Thank you for the vision and provision, even when I did not see how it would happen. Thank you for keeping your hand of protection on me. There is no greater love than the love of the Father.

To my husband Charles, thank you for your love, support and encouragement over the years. It means more than you will ever know. The glory of this latter **house** shall be greater than of the **former**, saith the Lord of hosts: and in this place will I give peace, saith the Lord of hosts (Haggai 2:9). You are a gift from God. I love you.

To my three mighty men of valor: Charles III, Carson and Caedan, you have been chosen for greatness. Walk worthy and do not look to the world for the things that God has placed in your hearts. Seek first His kingdom and His righteousness, and all these things will be given to you as well (Matthew 6:33). Love you, my three sons.

Thank you to my co-laborers in dance ministry for sharing your testimonies: Linease Bethea, Teresa Jones, Stephanie Knight and Rochelle (Shelly) Turner. Thank you to all who spoke an encouraging word or prayed for me during this process.

Called to Dance

A Dance Ministry Guidebook

Table of Contents

Foreword
Introduction

Foreword

God calls each of us to Himself. As we answer that call, He then calls us into service for Him. Paryn Wallace is more than qualified to speak on the call of God. She is an amazing, faithful and dedicated leader with great insight to be able to speak about the call of God for the minister of dance. She has a proven track record through her many years in the ministry. She is a leading voice for the ministry of dance. This outstanding book is relevant and necessary and will take each reader into a higher level of allowing God's blessings to flow into them and through them to other people. I highly recommend this book for anyone who has already answered the call or who was wondering about answering the call God has for them. Paryn is a visionary worshiper who understands God's divine plan and how it will unfold through answering the call. *Called To Dance* will compel you to take Godly actions to facilitate and advance the call of God in your life.

Dr. Pamela Hardy
Serving with Humility, Soaring with Excellence
Advancing the Kingdom!
www.drpamelahardy.org
www.eaglesiti.org
214-402-9647

Introduction

I urge you to live a life worthy of the calling you have received, **Ephesians 4:1**. I found this scripture several years ago when I was wondering about my call to ministry. I received a call from a friend, and she too was having her own preoccupation with life. My friend had just had a baby and felt as if she was "just" going to be a mother for the rest of her life. Her struggle was something I'm certain many of us experience at some point in our lives. My friend went on further to say that she did not know what her contribution is in life and that she was not doing anything, and actually said that she was not rich or famous or anything.

The counselor in me kicked in, and we had a discussion about *The Purpose Driven Life* by Rick Warren. I told her that I had read the book with my church years ago, and it would be a good starting point for her to start to put the pieces together to figure out what she should be doing. I also talked to her about how our purpose is where we are right now. Many times we look at people on television and other people and see their success and riches and wonder why those things are not happening for me. Well, what God has for you, is for you, and you can't look at other people to measure your own success. If God has you as a stay at home mother taking care of your infant son, then that is your present purpose. Sometimes we try to get ahead of ourselves and more importantly, ahead of God as we compare ourselves to others. Do you ever notice that the people on television with all the money and success have problems and issues just like you and me? The only difference is that our issues are not aired on Entertainment Tonight, TMZ and CNN. The bottom line is money, success, fame and fortune do not guarantee purpose.

I knew at that time what my purpose was, so I was not struggling there, but when I came across the scripture, to walk worthy of my calling, I felt like God was calling me to go to a deeper level in ministry. I asked the question in prayer, Lord how do I walk worthy of my calling and what is my calling? I knew that I was called to ministry and leadership but how would that calling manifest? In every organization and ministry I had participated in, I was eventually given a leadership role. So I know who I am, but God how do I use that gift in dance ministry? When I attended my first Gathering of the Eagles conference 2006, the Holy Spirit began speaking to me and as I started the Eagles International Training Institute and progressed in the assignments, my calling began to take shape. I heard clearly "Called to the Kingdom".

There is a call to walk worthy. I heard a very empowering message from Reverend LaRue at Princeton University some time ago. He said, and I agree, that God calls each of us into His service however, there is a misunderstood notion that only ministers of the gospel are called, and we do not act on the calling that we hear because we believe that only ministers are called to preach. We sometime have a tendency to think that if we are not called to preach, then God has not called us to anything. This is not true and so many people miss their service unto God because they feel this way. LaRue used the example of a lumber yard; there is a whole lot of material just lying around waiting to be built up into something beautiful. This lets us know that God has a work for all of us, and God has a way of calling us into His service. We know **Matthew 9:37**, the harvest is plentiful and the laborers are few, and dance ministry is no exception. There are many out their starting dance ministries and dancing in the church without the foundation of biblical dance, even in this day when there are countless conferences, workshops books and information available on the internet. We are *Called to Dance,* and so we must be prepared to teach biblically based, sound doctrine dance ministry. So this means we must heed the call if we are serious about our calling and service unto God.

Tryggve Mettinger in his book entitled *In Search of God* describes two types of call narratives. The first call comes from the throne room directly from God, and the person who is called answers immediately and obediently like in **Isaiah 6:1, 8**. In the year that King Uzziah died, I saw the Lord, high and exalted, seated on a throne; and the train of his robe filled the temple. [8] Then I heard the voice of the Lord saying, "Whom shall I send? And who will go for us?" And I said, "Here am I. Send me!" Some hear the call like Isaiah and answer immediately and obediently. The second type of call is more typical; God comes down to meet us in the realness of our lives and engages us in a divine encounter like he met Moses at the burning bush. God meets us where we are and steps into our life situation and changes all of our ideas and plans. The very thing that we are counting on in life He changes it, but there is no such thing as running from God. There are many times that we run from the calling of God only to get where we were going and God is there too.

So today the message to all of us is wherever God calls us, He provides for us. You may not know the call that God has over your life. It may be dance ministry or ministry in the marketplace, but whatever it is, God does have something for all of us to do. To paraphrase LaRue, God is not looking for us to walk around this universe all day everyday with nothing to do, with no call or claim on our lives, God has work for us to do and when God calls you to work, He promises that He will be with you and that is good news. Just think that He called Esther for such a time as this. He called a young Mary to bring the savior into the world. Don't worry about your age; He called Moses at the age of eighty. Don't worry about your finances, don't worry about your preparation, God will provide.

God is calling you. He is calling me. He is calling all of us higher, and that higher calling requires higher levels of obedience, sacrifice and lifestyle changes. As you read *Called to Dance*, allow God to speak to your calling in dance ministry. Allow God to equip you with the foundational materials provided in *Called to Dance* to promote growth, knowledge and elevation in dance ministry but more importantly a deeper relationship with HIM. You are **Called to Dance**!

Chapter 1
The Call

Ephesians 4:1
As a prisoner for the Lord, then, I urge you to live a life worthy of the calling you have received. (NIV)

How many of us have felt the call to do something? Or maybe we have gone through life or the past few years without knowing our calling or purpose or in life. In Ephesians 4:1, we are urged to live a life worthy of the calling that we have received but if we don't know what that calling is, how do we move forward in ministry or in life? Merriam Webster defines calling as a strong desire to spend your life doing a certain kind of work (such as religious work) and the work that a person does or should be doing.

What if that calling is ministry, dance ministry? Is dance ministry even a calling? Can one have that strong desire to spend his or her life in dance ministry? Well, I believe there is a calling in dance ministry and more importantly, if you chose to answer the call and the path of dance ministry, there is a charge to walk worthy of the calling that you have received.

My dance ministry call was simple, but it was a process that took many years to be fulfilled. Are all callings simple? Like Moses, you hear the voice of the Lord, and you simply follow those directives given by God. We all know that is not how it works. The call is complicated, and sometimes it takes years before the actual call comes to fruition.

I grew up in a small rural town near Greenwood, South Carolina, by the name of Hodges, you probably have not heard of it either. I grew up doing some of the things most little girls like to do. On Mondays I had piano lessons, I was a Brownie Scout and then there was dance. When I was in the second or third grade, my mother signed me up for baton lessons. I liked the physical movement that came with baton so much that after a short period of time, I asked to enroll in ballet, tap and jazz classes. Wasn't that every girl's dream, to dance and be a ballerina? The only problem I had at the time, were the Monday piano lessons. I loved twirling the baton, I loved tap and jazz and ballet grew on me. I loved moving around and expressing myself through physical movement and using my face to express emotions. This allowed me to tell a story and be expressive without saying anything. I was a little on the shy side, if the truth be told, and dancing was everything to me. Even now, I get emotional thinking about it. After all of the dance lessons and scout meetings that I enjoyed, there was still piano on Mondays. Did I mention that I had to practice the piano for thirty minutes a day and keep a log of those practices? It was bad, really bad, but out of respect for my mother and my parents in general, I stayed with the lessons until eleventh grade and then before my senior year in high school, I was allowed to finally stop taking piano lessons, but I continued with my dancing and baton twirling.

I also need to mention that I grew up in a Baptist Church, in the rural South. There was Sunday school, the Usher Board and Choir, no youth groups. I attended Flint Hill Missionary Baptist Church in Callison, South Carolina where my father was the Assistant Sunday School Superintendent, a Deacon and a Trustee. My mother was a Deaconess, an Usher, and a member of the Missionary Society. This information is important to my story because I grew up in a church that was very traditional and as a young girl, I knew there was more to God. Flint Hill was a good training ground, but despite that traditional setting, I could always sense that God was bigger than any of us could ever imagine. Yes, like most churches at that time, we had the traditional Christmas and Easter Programs after Sunday School and all the kids of all ages dressed in their best and gave the obligatory speeches copied and pasted from poem and play books of the season. The reason that I was made or encouraged to take those Monday piano lessons was so that I could play the piano in church, something that no one else was doing at the time. In my opinion, I became too old to give those speeches, but I was quickly informed by my mother that I was never too old to play the piano.

I believe that my calling started way back then. While I did play the piano at Easter, my song of choice was "The Old Rugged Cross" and my Christmas standard was "Silent Night", my heart was never with the piano. I would literally sit in church and dream of bringing my tape recorder and placing it on the steps leading up to the left side choir stand at Flint Hill and have my mother push the play button and I would dance from side to side in front of the "Do This In Remembrance of Me" wooden table just below the altar. I remember thinking that the table would not need to be moved, just pushed back a bit, enough for me to turn and leap in front of the congregation. I dreamed of the songs that I could dance to that would be fitting and allowed. Maybe I could dance to "Gonna Lay Down My Burdens" or I thought about a Shirley Caesar song. Her concerts were always moving to me as a child. You name the song, I dreamed of putting movement to it. I am certain that my thoughts and feelings were shared by many young people in the church before dance was so widely accepted. I did not understand why I could dance in talent shows at school, pageants, recitals and dance competitions but not dance in the church. I believe that even then, God saw my heart and desire to worship Him and orchestrated my steps so I would never forgot the desire I had at such an early age. I believe He knew my desire was to glorify Him in the dance, even though at the time I did not fully understand what glorifying God in dance really meant.

Well, I never stopped dancing. I was a dancer in college as a Carolina Coquette at the University of South Carolina. I continued taking dance classes while in college and graduate school. As a young professional at Benedict College, I attended dance classes with the college students and was the dance team advisor. It was only after getting married and having children that my schedule did not allow me to dance. But God is so amazing that while living in Greenwood years later and attending Grace Community Church, I was introduced to the Sign Language Ministry. This was the closest opportunity for Christian movement to a dance ministry and I loved it. I worked to learn sign language words and build a Christian vocabulary and I became very involved with this ministry. The desire to dance came back again during those days with such conviction and passion that I envisioned myself twirling and leaping across the stage and floor giving all that I had to God. Expressing myself through dance was what I wanted to do, yet I never spoke a word of this to anyone. It was only after moving to Atlanta, Georgia a few years later, that I was exposed to a dance ministry. I remember seeing dance ministry in the church we were visiting at the time and later we became members partly because of the dance ministry. I was in tears watching. This is what I had seen in my dreams. Not just ballet in the church, but expressive movements that signify adoration and glory to our God, just as I had envisioned it all those years ago as a little girl in the Baptist Church. This was my dream. I auditioned and joined the dance ministry.

I knew very little about dancing for God, and I did not learn anything about God in this dance ministry either. I only saw people craving attention to be seen by the leader and the better dancers being asked to dance up front while other less skilled dancers (who had a heart for God) were placed in the back and not included in outside ministry engagements because they were not good enough or at least that was the insinuation. Secret practices were held for the more skilled dancers and in the beginning I was not in this category. Members were pitted against other members for leadership positions by the director, and although I was pursuing dancing in the church, I was not learning about dance ministry. I found myself thinking like them, that I was a better dancer than some of the women, and "why was she given a solo part and I can dance just as good if not better than she can dance?" The focus was not on God and sometimes not even about dance. The leader would call different members and say, "I'm stepping down from the ministry soon, and I want you to be the leader", then after talking to other people, it would seem like that same call was made to about two or three other people, and they all thought they would be the leader. It was a time of chaos for the ministry, but it was going to be my first time ministering at our church on Sunday. I had gone out on a couple of outside engagements with the ministry, but I was finally about to make my dance debut in church in the midst of the crumbling dance ministry.

It was indeed a troubling time, and it was only by the grace of God, that the Pastor made the wise decision to shut down that ministry before I made my dance debut. The shutdown was by the grace of God because I was a mess. It was then and only then that I was able to take a look at myself and realize without a doubt my situation was not God. I had been infected with the same competitive spirit that these dancers had developed and I was not better than them by looking down on others who did not have a skilled background. I also came to recognize that I did know dance, but I did not know anything about dancing for God. Shutting that dance ministry down for that period of time allowed me to work on me and build a solid foundation with God in relation to dance.

Two things happened to me during that time that changed my life as it relates to dance ministry. The first was the night I auditioned for the ministry there was another young lady who auditioned with me, Teresa Jones. Teresa was not a formally trained dancer at the time, but she was and is the most anointed dancer I have ever seen. She is responsible for my growth in dance ministry. She took me around to many dance workshops, training classes and Friday night worship services where the dance was free flowing and men and women were allowed to express themselves in dance or with flags, streamers, banners, and tambourines. This was a world that I had never seen before nor did I know it existed. During these early days, I went everywhere I could where there was Christian dance. To this day, I have not had anyone pour into my life the way that Teresa did during those early days. She taught me about garments and the necessity for covering up, choreography technique, and I learned dance ministry leadership. The call involves serving and sharing your gift with others.

There were three of us who prayed together about our dance ministry. Janice Moton was a part of this trio, we prayed, we traveled to workshops, and we learned about God in dance ministry. This was the part I was missing and now I saw dance ministry differently. It was not for show, it was not about who was up front or who danced on the side closest to the Pastors so that they could see you dance. I no longer cared about any of those things. My focus was on praising God, and this was real.

The second event that changed my life was actually dancing again and discovering that I had a real relationship with God. The dance ministry started rehearsal again, and it was the same old mess all over again, but this time I was different. The first song we worked on was "Thank You" by Richard Smallwood. I ate, breathed, and lived this song. During dance rehearsal one night we did a run through of the song. It obviously was not good. We were yelled at and berated because we were not putting our all into it. The smartest thing the leader said at that time was, "We are going to do this song again and think of something you are thankful about and dance from that place of thankfulness." When the music started again this time, I did not care anything about anyone around me. I did not care if the movements were right; I danced that night from a place of relationship with God. I was thankful; thankful for the time that I was in a van at night in the snow on the side of a mountain and the van began to spin around and all I could see were trees down the mountain side and I called on the name of Jesus and closed my eyes and that van continued to spin and landed into the back side of the mountain and not down the mountain. I thought about the eighteen wheeler truck that came minutes after the van had stopped spinning, if that truck had come any earlier it would have hit the van and forced us down the snowcapped mountain into a night of nothing but trees. I thought about my three boys and that they were healthy, my husband who was loving and always supportive, and I thought about my Jesus dying on the cross. Oh my God, I lost it. I began to weep. It was like God was playing a movie right before my eyes, and I saw all the material things that I had lost including my childhood home, other houses, a million dollar business, land, and money, yet all I needed was to be thankful right now.

When the music stopped, I was in a place no one could understand. I was over taken by the Holy Spirit. Teresa was there that night, and she was the one who had to tell them that I was fine and that I was just in that thankful place and that God was at work in my life. I have ministered many times since that night and God has moved during the ministry, but I am always, always brought to tears when I think about that night and when I danced out of thankfulness and because I could see the goodness of God. Now, there is not a day that goes by that I am not thankful. The praise break goes right here!

We did minister "Thank You" during two church services and the ministry altered both of the services. When your heart is in the right place, God never fails to honor His promises. That rehearsal night and the Sunday ministry was truly my initial birth into the ministry of dance.

The ministry at this point was up and running and again the games, lies and the petty behavior resurfaced. This time all of the dancers were called in to meet with the Pastor. Dancers that had not been to practice in months showed up, people that we did not even know were still with the dance ministry showed up. That was the nature of the ministry at the time and it caused a great deal of tension. Dancers would only come to the last rehearsal before a Sunday ministry, but if other less polished members did the same, they were not allowed to minister on Sunday. I remember Teresa, Janice and I fasting and praying before that meeting because we were told that this was the night that everything would, "go down". The meeting was indeed a hot mess, but the Pastor, or I should say the God in the Pastor, saw through all of the lies, plots and schemes of the enemy and at the end of the meeting, I was asked to take an interim leadership position on the dance ministry. Yes, I said I was asked to assume the responsibilities of leading the dance ministry. The only reason that happened was that during that six month shut down, I had a major spiritual overhaul and God honored the changes I made. I know that this was about God getting it right in me and not about me being seen. When you accept any calling you have to know that it is never about you.

Well, even though the position was an interim leadership position, I prayed for direction and began the process of seeking how I could make this ministry glorify God. I ordered books, continued to attend dance conferences and local workshops and studied how to be an effective leader on the heels of my dance mentor, Teresa, to make sure I understood leadership and I saw it in action with her. We worked on dances together for the ministry, we searched for fabric and garments together, and we taught the ministry rehearsals together until the day she told me that God was calling her to move to Texas. Just as I was growing into my interim leadership position, the rug was snatched from under my feet. Everything I was learning and had learned was through and because of Teresa. I did everything in my power, and I do mean MY power to convince her to stay. I made sure she knew that she was leaving me in a bind and that the only reason that I was able to lead was because of her. In other words, everyone would all know I was a joke, if she left. I made sure she knew that she did not have a place to stay, a job, nothing in Texas. Here she had been unemployed for an extended period of time, I used every resource at the time to try and find her a job. When I say I did everything to keep her around, I did, but I mostly cried. I did not understand why God had given me this mentor who had taught me so much and now she decided to up and move to Texas. I was upset with her and God, especially when she politely asked me to STOP trying to talk her into staying and STOP trying to find her a job and STOP crying. OK, I eventually came around and I stopped but I was still salty, mostly from all of the tears I cried.

I remember one day in prayer, God whispered to me that He would never leave me or forsake me and only then did calmness come over me. I heard, "you are a leader and you will lead". At the same time I was having my calm moment with God, He gave Teresa a plan of action to assist me in tackling my fears. We worked with four or five of the dancers including myself in the ministry. We gave each of them a song to choreograph and we worked individually with them to review the choreography and for each song. I videotaped each dance and those ministry pieces would be our dance ministry each month for the next five or six months. I am a teacher by nature and I would either teach or assist in the teaching and the choreography and solve any blocking issues as they came up as we taught the dances to the members. This plan allowed me to accept the idea that I would eventually be alone in my leadership duties and responsibilities.

The Sunday before Teresa moved, she ministered "I Believe I Can Fly". The Pastors called her up to pray for her future success and ministry in Texas. I can say that was the loudest I have ever cried in my life. I cried not only because my mentor was leaving, but I cried because that song ministered to me. I was beginning to believe that I could fly.

Before the end of that year, one of the Pastors asked to see me. Of course, I was terrified; it was like being called into the principal's office. I was previously told that if you were called in to the Pastor's office, the ministry was in trouble and I would be subject to a verbal lashing like never before. I took a deep breath and opened the door, only to find a friendly ministry conversation. I was asked how things were going and if the ministry needed anything. I was told that the dance ministry was going well and that things seem to be on track after all of the previous turmoil, and I was offered the position of dance ministry leader. There was one other person who had been considered, she had been with the ministry for years, but she declined. It was official, I was now the leader.

I do believe God saw the time, hard work, effort and education that I put into my temporary position and elevated me. The minister of music came to our rehearsal that Tuesday night. He asked us to minister at the watch night service that would be held in a couple of weeks, and he announced to the ministry that Paryn Wallace would be the new dance ministry leader. Some clapped and hugged me and others looked like he had announced that the world was coming to an end. My leadership tenure started as soon as the minister of music walked out of the door. I had one dancer say, "Why did they pick you? You have not been here at this church as long as I have been here". Then, there was the one dancer who said, "I'm dancing next month, by myself." I said, "Really? Where?" She said, "I am dancing here at this church on that stage." The enemy is real, do you hear me? I had to let all of them know that I was asked to serve in this role, I did not go out seeking this and as long as I was the leader, we would be united and minister as a group. No one would ever decide that they would minister solo unless they were not a part of the ministry or the church. When I say I would not be the leader that I am today if I had not gone through that experience, it is the truth, the gospel truth. It was, "the best of times and the worst of times". As the interim leader, I never had a problem but as the chosen leader, I felt like I was fighting alligators with a spoon. I did say chosen leader.

Well, we made it to the time that we usually break for the summer. During that time, I read books, I still attended Friday night dance services when I could, I attended dance conferences and it was at one of those conferences that I met Apostle Pamela Hardy and learned about the Eagles International Training Institute. In the first year of the conference inception, I traveled alone to the conference in Columbus, Ohio. I did not know anyone. I met so many lovely women and men of God at that Gathering of the Eagles. During the conference teaching, the ministry of dance opened for me to enhance my leadership skills, learn how to really operate a dance ministry and be the spiritual covering for the dance ministry. When I came back, there was much work to be done. I revised the ministry procedures and established consistency in the ministry. I learned how to step up as the leader without fear of losing friends. I also learned the value of friendship while leading. As I learned, I taught the ministry. Although I still had doubts about my abilities, the ministry grew during this time.

I have shared my experiences with you because some of you are in a battle right now in your dance ministry. You maybe questioning your calling because of all of the turmoil and confusion that you are facing. You may know that you have been called to dance and even to lead but dance ministry has been a challenge for you, too. When God calls you, He has to make sure that you know your calling is real and that you are not dancing because your BFF is in the dance ministry or you are interested in dance ministry for exercise. When you answer and accept the call, God will begin to make sure your walk is worthy.

Chapter 2
Are you called?

Most Christians long to hear the voice of God. I have heard "the voice", those soft whispers only a few times throughout my life, but one of the most profound encounters with God's voice occurred during praise and worship one Sunday at the ministry where I serving as dance ministry leader. It was sweet worship; I was talking to the Lord with both my arms lifted high. It was a sweet conversation because I was just saying and repeating, "Lord, I love you", "Lord, I adore you", "You are worthy Lord", when I heard the following, "I have **called** you for such a time as this. I formed you in your mother's womb, and I remember when you were a little girl and wanted to dance before me. I am the reason you have danced all these years, I am the reason you learned ballet, tap and jazz to use for the **kingdom**. You doubt yourself but I see the leader in you. I have prepared your for this time". Then in a flash, my mind took me back to Flint Hill Baptist Church, and I saw the red carpet, I saw the tape recorder on the steps leading up to the choir stand and I saw that little girl dancing around the altar in front of the wooden table, and I began to weep. This was my calling into dance ministry. This is why the name of the dance ministry I started after graduating from the Eagles

International Training Institute is titled, "**Called** to the **Kingdom**". So in my heart, soul and spirit, I received my calling into dance ministry that day during praise and worship. There is a calling to dance ministry. Once you receive that call, the directive is clear, walk worthy of the calling you have received. Are you called to the kingdom?

How does God call us into His service? God calls us into His service first by way of salvation. The first requirement of the calling into his service whether you are a dancer, musician or greeter in the church is to be saved. **Romans 10:9** tell us that if you confess with your mouth the Lord Jesus and believe in your heart that God has raised Him from the dead, you will be saved. It is only after salvation that we become God's chosen priest, separated for service unto Him as outline in **Exodus 28:1-3**.

One who answered God's call and worshipped Him with all of his heart was David. David was a shepherd boy spent all of his time in the field tending sheep. He did not waste his time playing video games and watching reality TV, instead he became skillful with the slingshot and taught himself to play a variety of musical instruments that he made himself. It was during this period of David's life as a shepherd when he had minimal life responsibilities that David came to know God so intimately and during the long nights under the stars that he drew closer to God (Cornwall, 1998). David wrote in **Psalm 8:3-4,** [3] When I consider thy heavens, the work of thy fingers, the moon and the stars, which thou hast ordained; [4] What is man, that thou art mindful of him? and the son of man, that thou visitest him? David was called to use his slingshot proficiency to kill Goliath and to serve King Saul. David was also called and anointed as a leader and eventually became king. While David had his flaws, he excelled at many things to include; shepherd, musician, soldier, king, Psalm writer and poet. Most importantly, David is known for the call he accepted from God to be a worshipper after God's own heart and to have an intimate relationship with Him. David had a deep thirst and hunger for God and wrote in **Psalm 63:1**, [1] O God, thou *art* my God; early will I seek thee: my soul thirsteth for thee, my flesh longeth for thee in a dry and thirsty land, where no water is. David's greatest call of service came out of his desire to worship God by bringing the Art of the Covenant to Mt. Zion to the Tabernacle of David. In **I Chronicles 15:16**, King David accepted the call of God by revolutionizing "Davidic" worship where he, the Levitical priests, and all of Israel ministered unto God. David's worship was a response to God's call. David accepted God's call by singing songs, dancing and playing musical instruments all to the glory of God. As he celebrated God and exhorted others to join him, he celebrated with feasting and pageantry. "He worshipped God in the ritual of the Tabernacle of Moses, and he worshiped God in the free-form of the Tabernacle of David" (Cornwall, 1998). It was David who marched in procession before God and danced with all his might before the Ark and set an example and pattern of enthusiastic worship. David's processional became one of the most worshipful and intimate displays of glorifying God.

One of my favorite verses as it relates to dance ministry is **2 Samuel 6:22 (NIV),** David comes home after bringing the ark back and dancing out of his clothes and his wife Michal says to him that he, the King of Israel disgraced himself by dancing out of his clothes in front of everyone. David's response in verse 22 is, "I will become even more undignified than this, and I will be humiliated in my own eyes."

I want that passion! How many of you want that "undignified dance"? Do we really dance like David danced? Remember David was called and when you are called, worship becomes more than ministry on Sunday mornings, it becomes a lifestyle. Are you called to dance?

How were you Called to Dance Ministry?

How do you know you are called to dance ministry, God speaks to each of us differently. Regardless of how He does it, He has a way of making sure we know that He has called us to dance. I will share the testimonies of a few ministers I have labored with in ministry over the years and list some of the steps they suggest to use as a guide to discover your **Call to Dance**.

Minister Linease Bethea:
Initially, the call came through my Pastor. We did not have a dance ministry at Harvest and after consulting God about a ministry going forth, he asked me to pray about it and informed me that I was the one for the work. I reluctantly agreed in obedience – although felt very inadequate. I didn't see it clearly - until I was on my way to North Carolina - not even thinking about the dance ministry - and a song by Shekinah Glory was playing. The words to that song hit me hard in my spirit. My God had delivered me from a lifestyle headed for certain destruction and had kept me from danger. He is so worthy of all my praise and worship. I suddenly became very small and He was greatly magnified. I heard His voice so clearly that day. "There are people standing, ready, waiting, hungry for the Word who has a real desire to praise and worship me in dance. Hear and obey my man of God Linease. Many will be delivered and blessed through this ministry." In my insufficiency, He is sufficient. The real preparation began and I started absorbing all I could about the ministry through prayer, studying, reaching out to other ministries, attending conferences, etc. I thought that my call was in the administrative area of ministry because in the natural that's where I'm strong but God said NO - there's a greater work for you in the dance and teaching the Word. He uses those skills in the call on my life.

Minister Teresa Jones:
For me I was 19 years old and had been saved for about a year, I have always had a desire to please God and wanted him to use me but never saw in myself where God could use me at. Well one day I was at church and we had a guest speaker and his wife from Los Angles come to the ministry, before they came forth my pastor kind of prepped us for what we were about to witness, he said God had something for us that not many churches had the opportunity to experience, we were special and God wanted to expand our worship in him. With that said the male speaker came forth and begin to speak on the freedom of God and how the enemy had stolen a gift and art form that was valuable to the Church and introduced his wife, she came up and said nothing but a track started playing and I experience the presence of God like I'd never known before. As she was ministering in dance my heart cried out to God and said that's what I want to do Lord, before I could get that out of my thought she dance up to me, pulled me out in the aisle and begin to pray over me and spoke these words, "You will worship the Father in Dance....so get ready!", my life has never been the same since. This is how I knew that I knew, I was called to the ministry of dance.

Minister Stephanie Knight:
I would dance in my private time alone just me and God. There was a dance ministry at the church I attended at the time but I did not hear God calling me to join them. A couple years later I joined another church. One evening I was standing after service near two people who were talking about starting a dance ministry at my current church home. God spoke clearly right then and there and told me to tell them I would be there. I did not want to go but I knew it was God because I had no plans on dancing in public. God used the director at that time to pull out what I did not even know was in me.

Minister Rochelle (Shelly) Turner:
I was invited to view the prep at the church I currently attend. I began participating not long after that and found that the instructor was absent more than she was available. That was discouraging to me and I believe to others as well. So, I asked her if she would not mind if I fill in when she is not available just to keep the ministry moving....The rest is HIStory. Since I had never even heard of the ministry of dance, I hungered and thirsted for the **right**eousness in what is dance ministry and doors of learning (conferences, the Network, EITI) kept coming to me as I kept seeking them and still seek them.

Steps to the Call:

- Spend time with God in prayer and put your relationship with Him first.
- Study and know the word because dance is the Word in motion. This is the foundation you will need to stand.
- Have a passion for dance ministry.
- Would you be involved in dance ministry if there was nothing to gain other than your personal worship with the Lord?
- Check your motives for why you feel like dance is for you.
- Become a sponge for the ministry of dance and absorb all you can about the biblical foundations of dance. Attend conferences, read books, enroll in TEN, EITI or NLDN or other God driven networks.
- Reach out to others for mentoring. Take dance classes to build your dance vocabulary and spark your creativity.
- Your calling will come naturally, it is not forced although you will have to build, train and mature it by study to show yourself approved.
- Be quick to listen and slow to speak.

Chapter 3
Called to a Foundation

What is our foundation as a minister of dance? We are called to a higher standard as we move out in ministry and that begins with our foundation. Webster defines foundation as the basis or groundwork of anything, the act of founding, setting up or establishing. Not talent, not technique and not years of experience have anything to do with a good foundation in dance ministry. If not the aforementioned, then what is a good foundation for dance ministry?

Whenever I am called to assist a ministry and to teach dance, the only requirement is that everyone must bring a Bible or have the church provide Bibles for everyone. The strongest foundation for a dance minister to have is salvation in Jesus Christ. We are talking about dance ministry, but this is the case for any ministry in the church; you must be saved. I sometimes have some resistance from a few naysayers because they believe that dance ministry is a way to keep children and teens off the streets. I agree with that but if they are going to be off the streets and in the church, your church, and your dance ministry, they should be saved. This should be the standard for children, teens, and adults. I didn't say that the unsaved should not be in the church or participate in youth groups and other activities. I am saying that in order to participate in dance, greeter, choir, music ministry and other ministries where people's lives are directly affected, those members should be saved.

Romans 10:9 tell us "That if you confess with your mouth, Jesus is Lord and believe in your heart that God raised him from the dead, you will be saved." No one is too young, sometimes we tend to think children are too young but there is a standard. We should start early teaching the standard. We learn in **Romans 10:13**, for," Everyone who calls on the name of the Lord will be saved." Why saved? You may be thinking is this standard is just for dance ministry, the truth is you must be saved to get into the Kingdom of God, why should we lower the standard for dance ministry, or for any other ministry in the church for that matter. Salvation is foundational.

When it comes to foundation, we put more into activities of the world than what we do for the things of God. If we were going to play tennis, golf, or any sporting activity, or hobby for that matter, we would have to purchase all of the requirements for that activity prior to participating. My husband and I have three sons and over the years, the boys have participated in tennis, soccer, baseball, football, basketball, wrestling and track. For each of those activities they have had to learn the game, and attend a certain number of practices before they could play. We had to purchase equipment including, mouthpieces, shoes, socks, helmets, bats, gloves, shoulder pads, rackets etc. I could go on and on about the requirements and the costs of these items, but in order to walk on to the field or court, they were necessities to obtain. We knew the cost to play and we paid it.

When it comes to dance ministry, we often go before the body of Christ and the enemy without the biblical foundation necessary to minister before God's people. We don't know where dance is found in the Bible, if they danced in the Bible, or why it is important for us to dance today. We serve as dancing ministers and priests without the calling, without the training and the lifestyle necessary to glorify God. We go out each Sunday because we want to be seen, we don't focus on the ministry and the necessary foundation about dance, and we operate in dysfunction for years in our dance ministries because we would rather entertain than minister.

If your Pastor went into the pulpit each Sunday to preach without reading his Bible and studying the Word, there would be problems, right? If he never gave the church a scripture on any Sunday, if he never prayed or said anything half way spiritual, the people would eventually start to talk. We may not say anything it first couple of times but over a period of time, we would notice and would want some type of explanation.

It's the same with dance ministry, we sign up for dance ministry but in some cases we don't know anything about dance in the Bible. We don't take the time to learn about what God says about dance ministry. We don't attend dance ministry conferences, workshops, read books or even read the Word of God to learn about dance ministry. And, we don't know about garments and our role as ministers in dance ministry. We then wonder why our dance ministries are ineffective and dysfunctional, a simple answer, no biblical foundation. We are called to have a foundation in the Word.

Chapter 4
Called to Dance in the Old Testament

In order to build our foundation in dance ministry, we must begin our journey of dance in the Bible, starting with the Old Testament. Dance has a rich beginning and history in the Bible. The definition of dance is graceful, rhythmic movement in time to music. To the Jewish people, dance during biblical times meant to whirl, to spin, to leap and to jump. These Jewish descriptions are but a few of the terms used to describe dance in the Bible.

Just as dance is an important part of our worship experience in churches today, it was a significant part of Jewish culture during the Old Testament. In the Holman Bible Dictionary, Glenn McCoy states that dances were performed on both sacred and secular occasions, though the Hebrew mind would not likely have thought in these terms. McCoy states that there were eleven terms to describe the act of dance in the Old Testament. This leads us to believe that the Hebrews had an interest in dance.

One term used to describe dance suggested dances at holy days, feasts and in processional marches. Dance was also significant during the Old Testament by way of military victories and it was customary at weddings. Dancing most often occurred at religious celebrations as the Hebrews would praise God with music and dancing. Dance was primarily performed by women, but there were occasions when the men danced. Although it is noted that they did not dance in mixed groups and the dance of the Jewish people was similar to what we today call folk dance (Holman, 1991). *This symbol < > denotes the location of Hebrew and Greek words found in Strong's Concordance.

The first mention of dance in the Bible starts with the prophetess Miriam in **Exodus 15:20-21.** Miriam and all the other women went out to celebrate victory over Pharaoh's army at the Red Sea. These ladies led by Miriam had timbrels in their hands and danced and sang to celebrate their military victory. The definition of the type of dance by Miriam is called **mechowlah <H4246>**; this word means a dance, with dances, and in dances. These ladies led by Miriam were celebrating God's deliverance at the hand of their enemy. If dance had not been so important, Miriam and the other women would not have had their timbrels and other instruments of praise close at hand.

There is also the first mention of the type of worship desired by God. In **Exodus 5:1** Moses and Aaron asked for the release of their people specifically so that they could hold a feast and worship God. The Hebrew word **chagag <H2287>** means to celebrate a festival and to dance round and round in circles. Because dance was so important during the Old Testament, **Ecclesiastes 3:4** reminds that there is "a time to mourn, and a time to dance." So it was acceptable to dance. God in His infinite wisdom knew that there would be a time to dance. In **Ecclesiastes 3:4**, dance is **raqad <H7540>**, meaning to stamp or to spring about wildly for joy. So God, from the beginning of time created many different forms of worship to include dance, singing and the use of instruments to glorify Him. In her book entitled *Worship Him*, Fuchsia Pickett states that, "He made us with the purpose of satisfying the longing of our hearts for Him." He also knew that there would be a time to worship Him in the dance.

As mentioned earlier in **Exodus 5:1**, feasts and holy days were another important part the Jewish culture during the Old Testament that was celebrated with dancing. Even with the Passover's origin in **Exodus 12:15,** this was the start of a generational seven day celebration where dance was a part of the festivals in honor of God and out of their obedience to Him. The Hebrew word **chagag <H2287>** means to celebrate a festival and to hold a feast. Marriage celebrations were also another major part of the Jewish culture that included dance. At a marriage choosing ceremony in **Judges 21:21,** Jewish virgins were allowed to dance and the men took the virgins as wives while they were dancing. The Hebrew word for dance in this scripture is **mechowlah <H4246>,** meaning a dance, with dances and in dances. This dance is the same as Miriam's dance in **Exodus 15:20-21**.

As mentioned earlier, military victories which included dancing were also an important part of

Jewish culture during the Old Testament. Just as Miriam and the other Israelite women celebrated with their instruments and sang and danced after the triumph at the Red Sea, dancing celebrated other military victories. In **Judges 11:34**, Jephthah's daughter came out to greet her father after a victorious battle with timbrels and dances. When David returned home after killing the Philistines in **I Samuel 18: 6-7**, the women from all the towns of Israel greeted them with the joyful songs of singing, and dancing with musical instruments.

Scripture also supports that women were not the only dancers during biblical times. In **I Samuel 30:16**, we find the Amaliekite soldiers celebrating with eating, drinking and dancing after they captured all of the women and spoils at David's camp. David and his men, with the help of an Amalekite servant, captured them and took back their women and spoils. One cannot forget one of the most infamous dances in the Bible by King David. **II Samuel 6:14, 16** we have the ark being returned into Jerusalem and King David dances and leaps so much that his wife despised him in her heart. The dance by King David has two different meanings; **pazaz <H6339>** describes his leaping and also means to spring about as if separating the limbs. His dance is also described by the word **karar <H3769>** which means to whirl.

There are also scriptures in the Old Testament where dance is mentioned as an idolatrous act. In **Exodus 32:19**, in the story of the golden calf, the people worshipped and danced around this calf made from their jewelry, which angered Moses enough to make him break God's commands. In **I Kings 18:26**, an altar was made to worship Baal, and the people danced around the altar as they waited for Baal to answer them. So, as we see dance can come forth in an idolatrous act. It is clear from these few scriptures that dance was an important part of biblical times during the Old Testament.

In the Hebrew language there were only 8,000 words. Many of those words were used to describe dance and the type of movement associated with that particular dance. A few of the words have been used to describe dance as they relate to battles, feasts, religious celebrations, marriages and holy days. Other Hebrew words used to describe dance and dance movements include **alats <H5970>,** which means to rejoice, to jump for joy, exult. In scripture, alats is a demonstration of what is going on inside of us. In **I Samuel 2:1,** Hannah is rejoicing because God has given her a son, and she is no longer barren, and she has salvation through God.   Hannah was unashamed to express the praise on the inside she had for God in an outwardly manner. In **Psalm 2:11,** there is "rejoice and trembling". In this Psalm of exhortation, David admonishes earthly kings that it would be wise for them to serve the Lord with fear and rejoice with trembling as a righteous worshipper. Also in **Joel 2:21, 23,** the Israelites are told to "be glad and rejoice" and to "rejoice in the Lord". They were rejoicing because of the great things God had done for them, by restoring the land to be fertile again and for bringing them rain. In the Psalm and Joel passages, the Hebrew word for "rejoice and trembling" is the word **giyl <H 1523>** which means to rejoice, exult, be glad and to spin around with violent or sudden motion. In **Genesis 47:31**, Jacob worshipped God by bowing on his staff out of adoration of God. The Hebrew word for bow is **shachah <H7812>,** meaning to depress, to worship, bow, bowed down, prostrate oneself before superior in homage, before God in worship. This is exactly what Jacob did at 147 years of age before his death.

Once we realize that God is at the heart of the idea of worship and that we were created to have a relationship with God, our praise and worship of Him is taken to a new level when we include dance, music and singing. It is also important to know that the word dance was associated with worship and praise. The Old Testament is filled with exhortations to praise and worship God for His goodness as well as for His mighty acts (Pickett, 2000). In a look at **Psalm 149:3** "praise his name in the dance", this hallelujah Psalm is a hymn of praise to God, the Redeemer. It was probably written when David took over Zion and set up his government there. God is the center of our praise and our praises to Him should flow from our rejoicing hearts. Praise to God is shown in proclaiming His name, singing to Him and in dance with instruments. God takes pleasure in His children when they rejoice in Him. Also **Psalm 150:4** "and dance", this Psalm tells us what is needed to assist us in praising God; it was probably written for the Levites to get them stirred up in their praise. The Psalm emphasizes that God is the object of our worship because He is the Creator and Redeemer. Also because God is all that and because we have breath we praise Him. We were created to praise Him so with all the instruments and with dance, we give Him all the glory. In these scriptures, **machowl <H4234>** is the Hebrew word used to describe a round dance, to whirl, dance to symbolize joy.

As we explore worship in relation to dance, in the Old Testament it is God who initiates the worshipful response of the Israelite people by revealing his divine name, then rescuing Israel from its oppressors and establishing a covenant with them. Easton's Illustrated Dictionary relays that people acknowledged and worshipped God by attending the temple, offering sacrifices and participating in the annual festivals, feasts, religious ceremonies and holy days. As we have discussed earlier, the Hebrew word for keeping feasts, celebrate festivals, and to dance round and round in circles is **chagag <H2287>,** with this word there was some type of visible movement demonstrated. An example of this can be found in **Psalm 42:4,** the emphasis is keep holy day. In this scripture, David remembers all those good things that brought him into the presence of the Lord. He remembers the holy days, the three feasts held every year and the freedom he had to worship God in his own house when he was not exiled.

In a study of how the word praise is associated with dance during the Old Testaments, the International Standard Bible Encyclopedia defines praise as honor, reverence, homage, in thought, feeling or act, paid to men, angels, or other "spiritual" beings and figuratively to other entities, ideas, powers or qualities, but specifically and supremely to Deity, as in God. As an act of reverence to God, In **Exodus 4:31,** the elders bowed down. The elders saw and believed the miracles that Aaron spoke and Moses revealed, and because of their faith and reverence to God, God would deliver them from Egypt. The act, "bowed their head and worshipped" comes from the Hebrew word **shachah <7812>,** meaning to depress, to worship, bow, bow down, to depress, prostrate oneself before superior in homage, and before God in worship. Another example of this praise can be found in **Psalm 99:5,** this joyous Psalm of praise is to God because He is gracious and on the throne He is to be exulted and "worshiped at His footstool". The footstool they worshipped was probably a reference to the ark, where God's glory lived. In these and other Hebrew words we learn that our chief goal in life is to dedicate all that we have to God in everything that we do.

As we look at dance during the Old Testament biblical days, we do find a few similarities in the church today. The first is that, our dance in the church is God centered. Some of the movements are the same, like the spinning, leaping, and whirling.

I believe that there is going to be a true revival of dance in the church today but it is being held up in a spiritual realm by those who are still putting God in a box. The box that I am referring to is entertainment. So many people in the church today look at dance as something to entertain them before or after the preached word or as entertainment for their church programs. Many Christians today do not look at dance as scripture in movement because they are not being taught about the background and relevance of dance in the church. I have also found that many are not interested in learning about dance in the church. Instead they view it as a recital time or a time to be seen because "I have been dancing all my life". This view is distorted because God is not the focus.

In her article "The Significance of Dance: Why Satan is Dancing While the Church Drags Its Feet", Juliette Eyeman suggests dance is important to the church and that dance is being restored in the church today for several reasons to include, it adds visual aspect to worship and is universal across languages and cultures, it is the fulfillment of prophecy and a sign of blessing and restoration in the church. As we take a closer look at dance in the church today, it does add a visual aspect that is not entertainment but it is the preached word through movement and music. Today in our churches, God is using dance for healing, deliverance and breaking bondages off of congregants. As a fulfillment of prophecy, in **Jeremiah 31:13,** the church is referred to as the virgin will be restored and both old and young men will rejoice in dance, and God will turn their sorrow into joy. This "I will" prophecy from God is applicable to the church today. Dance is also universal across language barriers and cultural differences. Many times when language barriers exist, dance becomes the universal communicator. Even in our own country, dance in the church by way of mime and urban dance is reaching and breaking down cultural barriers while saving souls for Christ. God is using dance in the church as a sign of blessing and restoration. Lastly, God's word commands us in **Psalm 149:3** to "let them praise his name in the dance". We are reminded that though Satan has made the dance a sensual expression among the children of darkness, the dance belongs to the people of God and that God is restoring the dance to the church and to His people to worship and praise Him as He has commanded us to do (Pickett, 2000). Dance in the church will continue to be strengthened when we come together corporately in praise and worship to magnify Him.

Dance ministry is important in our churches today and dance is being restored in our churches as a fulfillment of God's prophecy and command to praise His name in the dance. Our worshipping hearts through dance, praise and worship will touch the heart of God.

Chapter 5
Called to Dance in the New Testament

As we continue in this biblical foundation journey in the New Testament, the words have changed to Greek, but the desire to praise, rejoice, worship and celebrate God through dance and movement has not changed. It is important to note how dance was a part of the everyday lifestyle and influenced everyday life activities in the New Testament. After 400 years of silence from God, the New Testament begins under Roman influence and follows the life and ministry of Jesus Christ. It is interesting to note that at first glance through the scriptures; one might consider that dance is not referenced as much in the New Testament as it was in the Old Testament. M. Daniels (1981) would suggest that there are more references to dance in the New Testament than originally thought due to the Aramaic language that the Jews spoke, the word for rejoice and dance had the same meaning. In the New Testament dance was a significant part of Jewish traditions and customs. Dance was deeply rooted in the New Testament believers and was still being celebrated at festivals and holy days, weddings and feasts and as a part of celebration and worship. R. Gagne (1984) proposes that the New Testament gives less direct references to dance without the need to mention it explicitly. Dance had become a part of their worship and everyday activities and because it was a part of who they were, there was not a need to mention it as much in the New Testament. This point of view is worth including because it does make sense, we know that festivals and celebrations did not cease during the biblical days of the New Testament.

Out of the several times dance was mentioned in the New Testament, the first mention of dance can be found in **Matthew 11:17**, when Jesus spoke to his adversaries and said, "We have piped unto you, and ye have not danced; we have mourned unto you, and ye have not lamented". Jesus was using the example of children dancing and playing by saying that nothing that neither her nor John the Baptist had done would satisfy them. Dance in this scripture is **orcheomai <G4640>,** meaning dance, to dance in rank or regular motion. There is also the first mention of movement in **Matthew 5: 12**, when Jesus said "Rejoice, and be exceeding glad; for great is your reward in heaven: for so persecuted they the prophets which were before you". The words rejoice and exceeding glad are words that indicate movements of excitement that are related to the word dance. Movement in this scripture is **agalliao <G 21>,** meaning glad (be; make), be exceeding glad, gladly, joy, joyfulness, joyfully, joyous, rejoice.

Dance, in the New Testament, is described by Greek names that imply worship and movement. In

Luke 15:25, dance is described as **chorus <G5525>**, primarily denoting an enclosure for dancing. It also means of uncertain derivation a ring, that is, round dance (choir) – dancing. The scriptural context for chorus found in **Luke 15:25**, is the very familiar parable of the lost son. "Now his elder son was in the field and as he came and drew nigh to the house, he heard musick and dancing". Dance in this scripture was a form of celebration for younger brother's safe return home. In another example of dance, **Matthew 14:6** reads "But when Herod's birthday was kept, the daughter of Herodias danced before them, and pleased Herod". Dance in this scripture was used as a form of entertainment for guests at Herod's birthday celebration. This was not a religious dance. Dance in this scripture is orcheomai.

There are a few other words used to describe dance in the New Testament, to include **skirtao <G4640>,** which mean leap, leap for joy. Similar to skairto (to skip); to jump, that is sympathetically move (as the quickening of a fetus). A scriptural example of skirtao can be found in **Luke 1:41,** when Mary visits her cousin Elisabeth "when Elisabeth heard the salutation of Mary, the babe leaped in her womb". Another Greek term used to describe movement in relation to dance and worship is **proskueno <G4352>,** meaning to prostrate oneself in homage (do reverence to, adore) worship, to fawn or crouch to. A scriptural context of proskueno can be found in **Matthew 2:2** in

43

Matthew's account of the birth of Jesus; the wise men came from the eat to worship Jesus. The Magi say, "Where is he that is born King of the Jews? For we have seen his star in the east, and are come to worship him." When the Magi found Jesus, according to custom they would lie prostrate by kneeling and putting their heads between their knees and have their foreheads touching the ground. This was an expression of religious reverence. These examples may not directly use the word dance but they all indicate some type of movement when demonstrated in worship.

As briefly discussed earlier, dance as it relates to worship during the New Testament was a part of the lifestyle and customs of the day just as it was during the Old Testament. Easton's Illustrated Dictionary points out that in the New Testament, the sacrificial system, temple and priesthood which kept open the lines of communication between God and the people despite their disobedience, were replaced by the sacrifice, holiness and priesthood of Christ. Focus was placed on the example and life of Christ and the fruit of the Spirit. It became less of a necessity for believers to worship God corporately in special places, or the presence of God and the spirit of God was present everywhere. Jesus says in **John 4:23-24**. "But the hour cometh, and now is, when the true worshippers shall worship the Father in spirit and in truth; for the Father seeketh such to worship him. God is a Spirit, and they that worship him

CALLED TO DANCE IN THE NEW TESTAMENT

must worship him in spirit and in truth". The most common meeting places for the church was in the homes of the early believers, Paul's greeting to believers in **Romans 16:5** reads, "Likewise greet the church that is in their house. Salute my well beloved Epaenetus, who is the first fruits of Achaia unto Christ". No longer was it necessary to observe the annual festivals or the Sabbath, for now all the days and times are equally holy in God's sight (Easton, 2005). More specifically, dance as a form of worship did not change but became incorporated into the smaller settings of the church. In the New Testament, worship became a lifestyle, something that could be done any place and anytime. This meant that the believers did not move in and out of worshipping God as they had previously at festivals and holy days but they were always worshipping God. For the early Christians having a common meal together was a regular part of their weekly corporate worship (Easton, 2005). In the Old Testament, while dance and worship were reserved for special occasions and festivals, in the New Testament, worship gradually became practiced in the common everyday life experiences of the believers.

Although now a lifestyle in the New Testament, the influence of dance can still be found at celebrations, games and secular events. The following scriptures although mentioned earlier are excellent examples of the influence of dance in everyday activities. In the familiar parable by Jesus,

Luke 15:25, says "Now his elder son was in the field' and he came and drew nigh to the house, he heard musick and dancing". The return of the prodigal son was celebrated with music and dancing. There is also a reference to dance as something children would do in town at the square or at a wedding. In **Matthew 11:17**, Jesus said "And saying, We have piped unto you, and ye have not danced; we have mourned unto you, and ye have not lamented." In this scripture dance is orcheomai, meaning dance or to dance from the rank like a regular motion.

There is an example of orcheomai that is probably the most controversial mention of dance in the Bible, the story of Salome's dance for Herod. During the New Testament, as stated in the Holman Bible, it was common to have dancers entertaining at royal courts in Hellenistic and Roman times and this practice is confirmed by the dance of Herodias' daughter, Salome. In **Matthew 14:6-11** and **Mark 6: 21-28**, Salome's legendary story is told. Because dance is sometimes misunderstood, Qan-Tuppim states "the original Greek word used in the New Testament account referred to Salome as a korasion, meaning a little girl not yet old enough to have breasts or menstruate. Also, the original Greek word used for the type of dancing performed by Salome is orxeomai, which not only means dance, but the playful goofing off of young children. Based on this, it is concluded that Salome was probably just an

CALLED TO DANCE IN THE NEW TESTAMENT

adorable small child, the Shirley Temple of her day. Furthermore, scripture states that Salome's performance merely "pleased" Herod. "Had the biblical authors wished to convey something lewd, they could have instead said that her dancing aroused him, or that he lusted after here; but the Greek word used here is aresko, which does not convey any kind of sensual titillation" (Qan-Tuppim, 2003). Many scholars have portrayed Salome's dance as evil and seductive, which leads to dance in the church being perceived as evil. From these scriptures, we see Salome's dance in the New Testament probably caused more controversy than David's dance in the Old Testament. The obvious difference between the two was the object or motivation behind the dances. Based on the aforementioned scriptures, we know that dance was a significant part of life and worship in the New Testament. The scriptures were inspiration from God, and I would like to believe that in the New Testament, God's focus was on spreading the gospel.

From the beginning of time, the object of dance was to worship and glorify God and the New Testament brings us to a different understanding of the meaning behind the use of the word worship as it relates to dance. In his book, *The Philosophy of Worship*, Dr. Judson Cornwall reveals how worship was built on from the Old to the New Testament, believing that God's revelation was progressively revealed in the Bible. New Testament believers

47

were given the person of Jesus Christ and the shed blood of Jesus Christ handled sin's guild, penalty, presence and power. New Testament worship was no longer in a temple but worship could be offered to God any time, any place and for any reason, and all the while under the covenant of grace, every day is special and all occasions can be holy (Cornwall, 1998). The person of Jesus Christ, not His performance, was the center of worship in the New Testament.

The New Testament way of worship led to rejoicing. As briefly mentioned, earlier, there were several words that coincided with dance in the New Testament. This is why dance is said to have more references in the New Testament than first thought because of the word rejoice, based on the Aramaic language the words had the same meaning (Daniels, 1981). It is hard to picture someone rejoicing while standing still and not moving. This is why rejoicing is connected to the movements relating to dance. From the announcement of the birth of Jesus to the revelation of His being seated in Heaven at the right hand of His Father, rejoicing and joy has been a dominate feature in the Bible (Cornwell, 1998). In **Matthew 2:10**, "When they saw the start, they rejoiced with exceeding great joy". The wise men worshipped Him with exceeding great joy. Jesus is the beginning and the end of our most supreme joys and that is why we rejoice. That is why we dance!

The relative importance of dance in the church today means being able to dance, worship, praise and rejoice in honor of God without priests atoning for our sins and to be able to worship God at any place and at any time. Jesus died on the cross so that we might worship Him in spirit and in truth **John 4:23-24**. This is why dance and worship is so important to the body of Christ. Those who are against dance in the New Testament church would have you to believe that dance was something that was done in the Old Testament and was not carried over or practiced in the New Testament. It is a mindset like this that causes God's true glory not to be revealed to the church. This is why restoring dance to the church today is so important, God will receive the glory.

As the current New Testament church and ministers of dance, we have to be God's feet to carry the gospel and to dance in celebration of God, to travail and do warfare for God and to preach the good news of God's work through dance. My ultimate joy comes from Christ dwelling in me and fulfilling His called purpose in me. The relative importance of dance and worship in the church today is that each of us has the opportunity to go before God. The command in **Psalm 150:6** says, "Let everything that hath breath praise the Lord. Praise ye the Lord". Even though thousands of years have passed and the church has gone though many reformations and transformation, one thing still remains to be true, God is everlasting and He nor his His Word has changed and will not change. Dance was and will always be significant to the body of Christ, and as dance continues to be restored in the church today, God will continue to reveal His divine glory in dance ministry to those who are called.

Chapter 6
Called to the Levitical Priesthood

A priest was one who officiated worship on behalf of God. In God's original plan, **Exodus 19: 4-6** affirms God's desire for Israel to become a kingdom of priest and a holy nation having access to Him. Israel forfeited the priesthood by sinning again and breaking the covenant He made with them at Mt. Sinai as outlined in **Exodus 19:5**. God then instituted Aaron and his sons in **Exodus 28:1** to function as priests. God's choice of Aaron was confirmed by Aaron's budded rod in **Numbers 17: 8**. Then God chose the Levites to serve Aaron in **Numbers 8:18-19** by saying "And I have taken the Levites in place of all the firstborn sons in Israel. [19] Of all the Israelites, I have given the Levites as gifts to Aaron and his sons to do the work at the Tent of Meeting on behalf of the Israelites and to make atonement for them so that no plague will strike the Israelites when they go near the sanctuary". As modern day priests, ministers of dance use the Levitical priesthood as a foundational pattern for ministry excellence.

As a mediator between God and man, priest performed ceremonies relating to the worship of God on behalf of the Israelite people. God established the Aaronic priesthood in **Exodus 28:1** which consisted of Aaron and his four sons. Also at this time God gave Moses the instructions for building the tabernacle. The Levitical order or priesthood derived from the tribe of Levi of which Aaron was a descendant. The Levities were chosen by God in **Numbers 3:5-14**, to provide ministry in the tabernacle while upholding their name Levi which meant joined unto or attached. The Levites were attached to God as they offered worship and service unto Him. David Levy in his book *The Tabernacle: Shadows of the Messiah,* states that God graciously provided the office of the priest so that the people, cut off from Him because of their sin, could have access to Him through a mediating priesthood. Hence, priest became a channel through which spiritual life was communicated. Being a part of the Levitical priesthood came with many duties and responsibilities. The office of priest was held only for those chosen by God and born into the tribe of Levi. **Leviticus 1:2-9**, **13:2-3**, **24:2-9** outlines the duties of the priests to include pronouncing the unclean with leprosy, they were responsible for the burnt offerings in the tabernacle to include the cleaning, killing and the sprinkling of the blood sacrifices. The priests also kept the continuous flow of olive oil burning in the candle sticks and baked the twelve cakes for the meal offering in the tabernacle. Their responsibilities were very detailed and important in their service unto the Lord in the tabernacle.

Although all priests were chosen from the tribe of Levi; they still had certain requirements to fulfill prior to entering the priesthood. They had to be at least 25 years old and had to have five years of training before being released as priests. They could also have no physical defects. The Levites were not fit for service in the tabernacle if they had the following: body blemishes, blindness, lameness, a flat nose, limbs that were deformed, a broken foot or hand, a hunchback, dwarfism, defective eyes, eczema, scabs or if they were eunuchs. These Levities were provided for even though they were rejected from service in the tabernacle. One might ask why were they rejected from service and what do their physical defects mean spiritually? **Leviticus 21:18- 21** states [18] For whatsoever man *he be* that hath a blemish, he shall not approach: a blind man, or a lame, or he that hath a flat nose, or anything superfluous, [19] Or a man that is brokenfooted, or brokenhanded, [20] Or crookbackt, or a dwarf, or that hath a blemish in his eye, or be scurvy, or scabbed, or hath his stones broken; [21] No man that hath a blemish of the seed of Aaron the priest shall come nigh to offer the offerings of the LORD made by fire: he hath a blemish; he shall not come nigh to offer the bread of his God.

The animals presented in the tabernacle sacrifices were without blemish because they each represented Christ who had no blemish in Him. In a closer look at each deformity, a blind man or a perhaps a man with one eye would not be able to carry forth the vision set by God. In her book, *The Royal Priesthood,* Dr. Pat Riley writes that one of the greatest tragedies to befall mankind is that some of us have sight but no vision and that God was revealing to us that a man that has no vision is not allowed to minister to Him behind the veil.

A lame man would not have the stable footing necessary for the job and would be impaired in the freedom of movement therefore unstable in his representation of Christ. One with a flat nose could have several meaning, the first could mean that they would spiritually be unable to smell the "sweet savour until the Lord" and therefore could not be a blessing to God in **Leviticus 1:9** "and the priest shall burn all on the altar, *to be* a burnt sacrifice, an offering made by fire, of a sweet savour unto the LORD". The flat nose could also mean one who was unable to perceive good and evil because their ability to discern was not fully developed. The superfluous meaning six fingers or extra toes could mean that these persons would add on to the duties and responsibilities more than what should be included in the tabernacle services. An example may be taking more into the tabernacle or doing more than the required amount of service. We know that Jesus was the right sacrifice for our sins and after Him nothing else was needed. **James 1:21** tells us to "wherefore lay apart all filthiness and superfluity of naughtiness, and receive with meekness and engrafted word, which is able to save your souls".

Many times in service, we act out of our deficiencies or lack. The broken footed represented one who is fragmented or broken into pieces; possibly meaning the person would be unfaithful ad undependable. The broken handed could represent a broken spirit or a person who is shattered or lacking power and direction. A person lacking power and direction would not be a true representation of God because everything He does is whole and complete. The crookback represents one who is deceitful, makes false claims, unable to stand the truth and cannot be trusted with the burdens of other and one who is unable to stand tall and walk upright before the Lord. The dwarf represents one of small statue, one who is under developed and still on baby food and not quite ready for the fullness of the Word. The blemish in the eye or protuberance of the eye or observable spots on the eye meaning one may only see faults and recognize them in others but not able to recognize them in his own life. Those with scurvy could mean those persons who are bitter, scornful or just plain mean and just need to submit to God and walk in the spirit. While those with scabs represent persons with bad habits or those with jealousy, and forgiveness who continue to pick at their sores and delay their healing. A eunuch or a person with broken stones means one with imperfect testicles as translated in the Living Bible.

This person cannot reproduce, is un-productive and incapable of being fruitful and replenishing the earth with life.

The persons with the deformities mentioned were still provided for because they were Levites but unable to approach the holy effects associated with the tabernacle. J. Vernon McGee's Thru the Bible (1984) states that there is a spiritual lesson for us as we look at the deformities; there are many believers who have some serious handicaps either physically, morally, ethically, or spiritually. Their deformities would exclude them from certain forms of service; yet they are still saints of God who have all the rights and privileges of everyday believers. As leaders in the church today, if we see any of these deformities in our lives, we must ask God to heal us and stay in His word so that we will be able to stand upright, be blameless and have a lifestyle that is pleasing to God.

Garments:
As the priesthood was to be without blemish, the garments of the priests had to also be in order and representative of their type of service unto the Lord. God gave Moses detailed descriptions on the garments to be worn by the priests. **Exodus 28:2** states and thou shalt make holy garments for Aaron thy brother for glory and for beauty. The garments were only to be worn by priests during their service in the Tabernacle. The garments were glorious in the eyes of the people because they

were representative of the priestly office. They were beautiful in color to harmonize with the furnishings of the Tabernacle. **Exodus 28:3** affirms that the garments of the priesthood could only be made by wise hearted; this meant the person making the garments had received from God special knowledge and skill through the Holy Spirit to make these garments.

The garments were so important that God through the scripture describes in detail how each item of clothing was to be make. Each piece of clothing is full of divine truth and spiritual teaching typical of the Lord and His ministry (Levy, 2013). Each piece of garment was made with fine fabrics with colors and trim that were representative of the deity of God and were a symbol of the righteousness and holiness of Christ. The breeches, were made out of linen because linen does not sweat, were worn so that the secret parts which symbolized righteousness were covered. The coat of righteousness worn by the high priest had three layers and represented the righteousness of Christ and His perfection, holiness, justice and faithfulness. The heavenly blue robe spoke of the authority of the High Priest, the Levitical priest did not wear this blue coat. The bell and the pomegranate at the hem of the robe represented the gifts of the spirit and the fruit of the spirit and if the priest did not move and you could not hear the sounds from the robe, this represented a dead priest. If we as dancing priests today do not move and have visible fruit in our lives, we too will die spiritually. The ephod, the most colorful part of the garment spoke of holiness and beauty. The shoulder stones representing governmental authority named each of the twelve tribes by birth order and were placed on the shoulders of the High Priests representing they bore the weight of all Israel but **Isaiah 9:6** tell us that Jesus will have the government on His shoulders. The breastplate had twelve precious stones representing each of the twelve tribes worn over the heart of the priest represented how God loves us all. The Urim and Thurmmim represented the gift of prophecy with truth and light. Finally the crown of glory or mitre represented being crowned with His glory. God was very careful that every garment painted a portrait of His beloved Son and it had to be done to perfection because not only is Christ the tabernacle, but Christ is the Eternal High Priest (Riley, 2006).

Serving as New Testament priests and ministers of dance in the God's house comes with many responsibilities. Just as garments were important to the Levitical Priesthood, our garments are an important part of our priestly ministry. Our garments are a symbol of our righteousness. Just as the garments worn by priests indicated that they were chosen by God, our garments should be chosen by us to bring glory to God. Spiritually we have been clothed in the white garment of salvation and robed in righteousness. Our garments are important to us because they keep us from coming in contact with the corruption of the world, the things that can spot us if it touches our flesh. Even as dancing priest; I believe that our garments say something about our relationship with God. There are those who dance before the Lord in worldly clothing, showing more than what needs to be seen, these persons are indicating their lack of relationship with God. Spiritually our garments say even more about the life we are living for Christ. I know people who categorize parts of their wardrobe as "church clothes", I always explain to them that all of my clothes are "church clothes" and there is not one thing in my closet that I cannot wear to church at any event. As called ministers of dance, we cannot pick and choose whether or not we will wear our "church clothes" today. Every day is a church day, it is simply a matter of lifestyle.

Today as responsible New Testament priests, our first role is the same as the priests in the Levitical Priesthood; we are to be holy and righteous as we minister unto the Lord. **Psalm 22:3** testifies "but thou are holy, O thou that inhabitest the praises of Israel". As the current New Testament priesthood, we draw closer to God through our worship. As believers, we have entered into a new covenant priesthood that is being fulfilled in the church. In our role as responsible priests we are to offer up spiritual sacrifices as stated in **I Peter 2:5.** Easton's

Illustrated Dictionary implies that now the term priest applies to all believers as we all have free access into the holiest of all and offer up sacrifices of praise and thanksgiving, and the sacrifices of grateful service from day to day. We are able to do this because of **I Peter 2:9** "But ye are a chosen generation, a royal priesthood, a holy nation, a peculiar people; that ye should shew forth the praises of him who hath called you out of darkness into his marvelous light". God made us kings and priests in **Revelation 1:5-6**, and when Jesus died on the cross, and the veil was torn from top to bottom, all believers were instituted into the New Testament priesthood by the blood of Jesus. Our response to our role as responsible priests is to offer the spiritual sacrifices of praise and worship. **Hebrews 13:15** affirms "By him therefore let us offer the sacrifice of praise to God continually, that is, the fruit of our lips giving thanks to his name". Consequently our responsibilities as priests have not changed. The only thing that we do not do is offer animal sacrifices; Jesus became the ultimate sacrifice, our Lamb of God. As priests today we often follow the pattern of praise outlined in the book of Psalms in our priestly ministry by praising with our hands by lifting, clapping and playing musical instruments. Lastly, we praise with our bodies by standing, bowing or kneeling and my favorite, dancing. We offer our bodies as living and holy sacrifice as outline in **Romans 12:1** and this is our reasonable spiritual service of worship. What an awesome responsibility to be chosen by God into His priesthood!

Our conduct goes hand in hand with our garments and our spiritual sacrifices of praise and worship. Just as it was mandatory for the priests to make wise choices about marriages and their families, we also have to make wise choices and strive for excellence in our lives at all times. We have some new converts in our church who have indicated to me that they are interested in the dance ministry. My response was positive however, I always begin talking about the dance ministry by conveying to them they training that is involved in the dance ministry, because we cannot bring of the flesh before the Lord and when I know you were at the club last night and you come to the church smelling like cigarettes, that's is not the "sweet savour" that God is look for in us and that tells me that you are not ready for the dance ministry. We cannot come to church bursting out of our clothes because they are too tight or too short or just plain inappropriate and expect to dance before God; our lifestyle must indicate that we have a relationship with God for real. When we do minister unto the Lord, we cannot wear any old something just so we can be seen. We need to bring to God what He brings to us, His holiness and righteousness and His excellence. This is why our garments, our conduct, and the lifestyle that we represent as priests must be presented in excellence. That is not to say that we are perfect because we die to ourselves daily and wrap ourselves in the Word. We have been clothed in His righteousness are fit for His worship and service because when we are to go forth from worship to service in this dark world we manifest the glory and beauty of Christ through our lives (Levy, 2013).

The Levitical Priesthood parallels our current ministry. The first parallel is that as Aaron was called into the priesthood, in **I Peter 2:9**, the church is called a kingdom of priests. Secondly, a man had to be born into the priesthood. We are born-again believers of the priesthood adopted into the family of God with all rights and privileges of the Son. Lastly, all of Aaron's sons and descendants were secure in their position as priests based on God's appointment of Aaron. **Romans 8:35-39** qualifies us as believer priests secure in Christ, and we will not be separated from Him or the priesthood. Each of the priesthood qualifications; from the sacrifices to our conduct as priests is to bring honor and glory to God by praising Him. Even our garments are important to our ministry because they fit our office and represent Christ. Our role as believer priests is one the Israelites were not able to experience or image, we can all worship before the throne to give Him praise and to glorify His name without the barriers but with direct and complete access to God through Jesus Christ.

Chapter 7
Called to Worship

"To worship you I live, To worship you I live, To worship you I live, I live, I live, To worship you". These are the words from song writer and worshipper, Israel Houghton. These lyrics express our true purpose and reason for living and operating in our call to dance, and worship the creator. Dance ministry is all about worship. We are called to worship. Only when we surrender our hearts to God and give Him total control of our lives do we know the true meaning of worship. There are many ways in which to express our calling to surrender to God, dance, music, instruments and singing are be a few examples of worship worthy of mention. These forms of worship, or as I would like to refer to them, as expressions of worship were introduced in the Old Testament and were passed down as tradition to the New Testament.

As we explore the meaning of worship, we see that worship is an act of honor, praise and reverence of deity. As learned from previous chapters, the Old and New Testament studies, worship meant many things to include shachah (to worship, bow, and prostrate oneself) and proskueno (to prostrate oneself in homage, worship). We were born with a desire and calling to worship God. (Cornwall, 1998) states that God desires our worship far more than we desire to worship Him and though the Bible He requires our worship, then He entices and inspires us to worship Him. What an awesome revelation to know that God desires me to worship Him and that He is delighted in my praises. God is delighted in our worship because He is awesome, He is omnipresent, He is worthy and He is love and He is worth worshipping. For this reason, we do not have a

spiritual life if we do not worship. Not only is it scriptural to worship God but worship nurtures and sustains the life God gave us when we were saved and without worship, the human spirit withers and dies (Cornwall, 1998). For all of these reasons, worship is just as significant in our lives today as it was in the lives of the believers during the days before, during and after the reign of Jesus Christ.

Starting in the Old Testament, biblical worship among God's people included walking with Him, being righteous and faithful before Him and building altars and temples in which to worship Him. Israel also started to worship God with dance, music, instruments and singing. These expressions of worship became a significant part of Jewish culture and religious celebrations during the Old Testament. As we look further at worship, dance was used to worship and celebrate God. **Exodus 15:20** [20] Then Miriam the prophetess, Aaron's sister, took a tambourine in her hand, and all the women followed her, with tambourines and dancing. **Mechowlah <H4246>** meaning a dance is the name of the type of dance led by Miriam. Dance was also included in feasts and holy days. In **Exodus 5:1**[1] Afterward Moses and Aaron went to Pharaoh and said, This is what the LORD, the God of Israel says; Let my people go, so that they may hold a festival to me in the desert. **Chagag <H2287>** means to celebrate a festival and to dance round in circles. Moses and Aaron asked for the release of their people so that they could hold a feast and worship God. The most familiar mention of dance in the Old Testament was when the ark was brought into Jerusalem. **2 Samuel 6:14, 16** reads [14] David, wearing a linen ephod, danced before the LORD with all his might, [16] As the ark of the LORD was entering the City of David, Michal daughter of Saul watched from a window. And when she saw King David leaping and dancing before the LORD, she despised him in her heart. In this scripture, dance is to leap called **pazaz <H6339> and karar <H3769>** which means to whirl. In the Old Testament, dance as worship was very much a part of the custom and lifestyle of that day. Dance was expressed with joy and praise as it was rendered unto the Lord.

As worship evolved and included music and instruments, God's presence was evoked even the more. The first mention of music and instruments can be found in **Genesis 4:21,** [21] His brother's name was Jubal; he was the father of all who play the harp and flute. In this scripture, Jubal was the father of all who played the pipe and lyre. Matthew Henry's Commentary describes Jubal as a famous musician, particularly an organist, and the first person who made rules for the noble art of science of music. Several of the Israelite prophets were musicians, we have already discussed Miriam and how she led the other women with timbrels, singing and dancing. Isaiah, the prophet, composed songs. In **Isaiah 26: 1-6,** his song celebrated the deliverance of all those who put their trust in the Lord. Then we look at David who was a warrior, King, and dancer. Richard C. Leonard mentions King David in his article, "Music and Worship in the Bible", by saying David established the place of music in the worship of God even before the sacrifices had been moved to Jerusalem. David instructed the Levitical musicians to celebrate the ark's journey to Zion in **I Chronicles 15:16-21**, David also appointed Asaph in **I Chronicles 16:1-7** as his chief musician who took care of continuous praise and thanksgiving music in the temple. In the temple, music was offered as a sacrifice of praise and became a regular part of the service. "The titles of fifty-five Psalms refer to the music director, with instruction for performance on various instruments or using certain tunes" (Leonard, 1997). There were also guilds of musicians, like the sons of Korah, who were dedicated to the discipline of liturgical music. In most cases music included vocals and instruments together.

As we look at the musical instruments, the most frequently named instrument in the Bible is the shophar, the ram's horn. The shophar which is often translated as the trumpet served as a signaling instrument in times of war and peach" (Holman, 1991). Examples of the shophar can be found in **Judges 3:27, Judges 6:34 and Nehemiah 4:18-20.** The shophar was also the most used instrument in the Old Testament, it was used in celebrations, for the announcing of the Sabbaths and new moons, used to warn of dancer approaching and to signal the death of kings and those in high governmental status. The shophar is still used in synagogues today. The lyre or **kinnor <H3658>** is a musical instrument with strings similar to a harp. David employed the use of the lyre by the Levities in worship; it was more often used to accompany those who were singing. Its shape was rectangle or trapezoidal and the number of strings on a lyre could vary by instrument. Other musical instruments referenced in the Old Testament were the timbrel or tambourine. The tabret is mentioned in **Genesis 31:27** and the timbrel was used by Miriam in **Exodus 15:20-21.** Flute or woodwind instruments call the Khalil was a popular instruments instrument but its uses were mainly associated with secular celebrations of funerals. Mention of the horn and trumpet can be found in **I Kings 1:39-40** and in **Jeremiah 48:36** there is reference of pipes. Music in Old Testament was an important part of the worship based on the numerous scriptures and the many inclusions of music as a part of worship experiences.

Many of the instruments discussed were played while people were singing. In the Old Testament, singing meant to sing, shout or cry out. An example of this is the word **ranan <H7442>** which means to chant or sing. Vine's Expository Dictionary of the Old and New Testament says that ranan occurs approximately fifty times in the Hebrew Old Testament with about half of those used being in the book of Psalms, where there is special emphasis on singing and shouting praises to God. In **Leviticus 9:24**, the word ranan is used for the first time when Aaron and his brothers were consecrated into the priesthood, the people shouted and fell on their faces when the sacrifice was consumed with fire. It should also be noted that psalms are songs with instrumental accompaniment. Other examples of singing can be found **in II Chronicles 5:12-14** in a description of the opening of the temple built by King Solomon.

> [12] **All the Levites who were musicians-- Asaph, Heman, Jeduthun and their sons and relatives--stood on the east side of the altar, dressed in fine linen and playing cymbals, harps and lyres. They were accompanied by 120 priests sounding trumpets.** [13] **The trumpeters and singers joined in unison, as with one voice, to give**

praise and thanks to the LORD. Accompanied by trumpets, cymbals and other instruments, they raised their voices in praise to the LORD and sang: "He is good; his love endures forever." Then the temple of the LORD was filled with a cloud, [14] and the priests could not perform their service because of the cloud, for the glory of the LORD filled the temple of God.

What a song! The worship was so powerful that the priests could not minister because the cloud of glory of God filled the house of God. So not only was there dance, music, instruments and singing in the Old Testament, these worship expressions were used in such a way that they were very effective and pleasing to God.

As we transition to the New Testament and look at dance, music, instruments and singing in worship, it should be noted that the worship of the emerging Christian movement did not produce new forms of music but shared the characteristics of music in the Old Testament, many of which are still found in the liturgies and clearly the worship life of the early church included psalms and other forms of song (Leonard, 1997). So the same expressions of worship in the Old Testament were transferred to the New Testament. In her book entitled *Worship Him* by Fuchsia Pickett, she adds that it would be too great an assumption to consider that all the Old Testament worship forms were somehow abolished for the New Testament Christians, even though there were no explicit instructions for them to be eliminated. Just as scriptures were written in the Old Testament and quoted verbatim in the New Testament, the same holds true for many worship traditions.

As we glance at dance in the New Testament, we know that dance continued to be a part of the lives of the believers and was being celebrated as part of worship, festivals, feasts, weddings and holy days. R. Gagne proposed that the New Testament gives less direct reference to dance but says that this points to a possible parallel of the Jewish tradition of presuming the presence of dance without the need to mention it explicitly. Dance became a part of the everyday lifestyle of worship in the New Testament and could be offered to God any time, place or reason. Dancing along with music can be found in **Luke 15:25**, in the parable of the lost sons at the celebration of the younger brother's safe return home. Dance in this scripture is referred to as **chorus <G5525>** denoting an enclosure for dancing. Also in the New Testament, the word rejoice is connected to the movements relating to dance. The focus of the New Testament was being able to worship in dance and rejoice in honor of God and adoration of Him without priests atoning for sins while knowing that Jesus died on the cross so that He would be worshipped in spirit and truth as stated in **John 4:23-24**.

In the New Testament, worship in spirit and truth included musical instruments. Instruments mentioned in **I Corinthians 13:1** included the pipes (flute), lyre (harp), cymbals and the trumpet. These instruments were commonly used at weddings and other joyous celebrations. In **Revelation 5:8**, there were harps used as instruments of praise in the vision recorded by John. In the singing of Psalms, the harp was the traditional instrument played with singing. The mention of musical instruments in worship is not mentioned in detail but, whereas many scriptures in the New Testament keep us singing as a gospel ordinance, none provide for the keeping up of music and dancing (Henry, 2008). In a similar account, The Complete Book of Everyday Christianity (Stevens et al., 1997) notes that the New Testament had very little to say about music but nevertheless, it is clear that music is a universal gift from God without which our world, as well as our worship, would be greatly impoverished. We do know that music did exist and was important in worship of New Testament believers.

While the New Testament does not include a lot of detailed information in reference to the use of musical instruments in worship, there are several scriptures about singing the praises of God throughout the New Testament. **Ephesians 5:19**, says that singing of psalms and hymns are for God's glory and is an ordinance of the gospel. John records in **Revelation 5:11**, [11] Then I looked and heard the voice of many angels, numbering thousands upon thousands, and ten thousand times ten thousand. They encircled the throne and the living creatures and the elders. These angels unite in song giving praises to the Lab because He is worthy. The New Testament also records that Jesus and the disciples sang a hymn after the Last Supper in **Matthew 26:30** and in **Mark 14:26** as part of the Passover tradition. Another example of singing in scripture can be found in **Acts 16:25** when Paul and Silas were singing in prison when the earthquake occurred. Even in the midst of the circumstances, Paul and Silas sang and praised God to point where they were delivered, and they brought salvation to the jailer and his entire household. Paul also taught New Testament believers that music should be a part of their worship life, in **Ephesians 5:18-19**, Paul was confident that "the point of overflow for the Spirit is singing" (Cornwall, 1998). These are but a few powerful examples of singing in the New Testament. Based on these scriptures and many others we know that worship traditions from Old Testament were passed on to the New Testament and did include music with instruments, singing and dancing. These expressions of worship continued to become an integral part of the worship lifestyle of the Christian movement in the New Testament.

The expressions of worship that we have discussed support each other throughout the entire Bible. As we bring honor and pleasure to

God through dance, singing and instruments it is important to note the significance of their relationship in worship throughout the Bible. When expressed corporately, these expressions of worship fulfill a supernatural dynamic part of worship described in the scriptures that reveal God's presence in a special way. The significance of the relationship whether these forms of worship are expressed individually or corporately is that they magnify and bring honor and glory to God. Every biblical expression of worship has its place and can be cultivated for the building and edifying of the body of Christ (Pickett, 2000). Throughout the Bible, as God is worshipped in spirit and in truth. The worship experience through singing, music or dance brings about a special reverence to God. This is seen in scripture when the presence of God filled Solomon's temple and the glory of God fell and the tabernacle was filled with joy and rejoicing. The true significance of the believer's relationship in worship is that God receives the glory and the biblical believers were in fellowship and relationship with the God who created them to worship Him. So the significance of the worship relationship is complete no matter the expression of worship, as long as we worship Him in spirit and truth with sincere hearts.

When we bow in reverence to God or if we worship God with dancing, singing, music and instruments, our worship will strengthen our faith as we touch the heart of God. Dance, music, instruments and singing are biblical expressions of worship that can be utilized in any worship experience as they magnify and glorify God. From the believers in the Old Testament to those of the New Testament, God created and called all of us to have a desire to worship Him. The expressions of worship only bring us into a deeper reverence of God as we worship Him. When worship is our true priority, we too can have the worship experiences of the Bible when the glory of the Lord fell and the worship touched the heart of God. We are called to dance and we are called to worship. God's desire is that we use as many expressions of worship necessary to walk in our calling to worship. "To worship you I live. To worship you I live. To worship I live, I live, I live, to worship you".

Chapter 8
Called to Start a Dance Ministry

The dance ministry is one of the most powerful ministries in the church. Any person or church interested in starting a dance ministry, and this includes community dance groups, must be mindful that before any rehearsals are held, any ministry songs selected or any garments purchased, there must be much prayer and fasting. After you seek and hear from God the work begins. As ministers of dance, when we are called to start a dance ministry, we are not going to just throw something together and expect God to accept it. God expects our best and requires our sacrifice to be excellent.

There are a couple of scenarios to consider. If you are interested in starting a dance ministry, don't just have a meeting with your pastor to say that you "would like to start a dance ministry". Do your homework before any meetings are held. If your church has never had a dance ministry or if the ministry has not been active for a period of time, a great deal of work must be completed. First, as the leader, do you have a relationship with God? Remember dance ministry is not about dancing. It's really about a relationship and lifestyle. The bible reminds us in **2 Timothy 2:15** [15] Study to shew thyself approved unto God, a workman that needeth not to be ashamed, rightly dividing the word of truth. This means that you need to learn and immerse yourself with everything you can to learn all you can about dance ministry. I mentioned in a previous chapter how I surrounded myself with more experienced ministers of dance, I attended conferences, ordered all of the books I could find and I enrolled in a one year intensive program- EITI (Eagles International Training Institute) and I have been studying and learning ever since that time to the present and I will continue to study and learn. There is nothing more important than continuous growth and development in ministry.

I once worked with a dance ministry where the leader had reached her capacity. This leader had only participated in dance ministry at a previous church and when asked if the new church had a dance ministry, was placed in a leadership role as the dance ministry leader. Please hear me in love, everyone is not called to lead. So in two years as the leader of this dance ministry, the leader had not taken a dance class, attended a conference, purchased a book or engaged in any type of dance workshops in the area that would be beneficial as the leader of the ministry or to the dance ministry as a whole. The leader did not want to co-lead in the ministry with a seasoned dance minister or step down to let someone else lead the ministry. She did not want to lose the title as dance ministry leader. This is all about studying to show yourself approved, because you are called. Before you walk into the Pastor's office or the meet with the Worship Arts Director about dance ministry, make sure you know everything there is to know about dance ministry and more importantly dance in the Bible.

Another scenario to consider if there is a dance ministry at your church but, it is not functioning in excellence. This is the case for many ministries who started out with just a few people and now has grown and people from various backgrounds and skill levels even maturity in Christ are in the ministry and the ministry has gotten off track. I have a passion for working with this type of dance ministry. What I have learned over the years is that this type of ministry has been operating in dysfunction so long, it is hard to get back on track and outside assistance is sometimes needed. Again the ministry and leaders need to be in prayer to find the right person to assist them. Getting on track requires change and the entire ministry needs to be prepared to change in some way. James Richards in his book *Grace: The Power to Change,* acknowledges that probably the greatest frustration among serious believers is the inability to change. He goes on to say that changes are often short-lived and many believers fall back into previous patterns of bondage. Dance ministry is no exception. I have found over the years that initially everyone wants their ministry to grow and be productive but when they have to make changes such as come on time to rehearsals, be accountable and submit to the leader, it is easier to fall back into old patterns of dysfunction. Change can be embraced as growth and growth needs stability and a solid foundation.

This is why every dance ministry has to have a solid foundation. There are several items that must be in place to build this solid foundation and bring stability to the dance ministry. Those items are: your church mission statement, your dance ministry mission statement, standard operating procedures for the ministry and the duties and responsibilities of the leaders. Let's take a closer look at each foundational piece.

Mission of the Church.
Before you start a dance ministry, make sure you know the mission of your church and the vision of the Pastor. Every church has a mission and it is usually printed in church materials. One church I attended, the church mission was to "Revive, Restore and Redeem". The vision of the Pastor was to revive, restore and redeem lost and hurting people back to the kingdom of God. A church mission statement is a formal summary that describes the aims and values of your church. A mission statement is instrumental to your dance ministry. Every member of your ministry should know the mission of the church and that mission needs to be engraved in everyone's heart.

Vision of the Dance Ministry.
The dance ministry is responsible for bringing forth the message that reveals and communicates the Word of God through an outward expression of creative movements. Your dance ministry should have a vision statement. That vision should be in conjunction with the mission of the church. Each dancer should know the vision of dance ministry and the entire ministry should operate, function and minister based on the vision. At every opportunity the vision should be communicated. **Proverbs 29:18,** reminds us where there is no vision, the people perish: but he that keepeth the law, happy is he. When the entire ministry knows the vision of the dance ministry and everyone is on one accord, God will receive all the glory.

Standard Operating Procedure.
Every dance ministry should have a Standard Operating Procedure (SOP). The SOP is a clear cut guide that explains what is expected of each dance ministry member. It sets the standard for how the ministry will operate. The SOP also outlines specific procedures about how to handle certain situations and operation of the dance ministry. The SOP is usually written by the dance ministry leader, worship arts director or executive pastor and approved by the pastor. It is usually reviewed and updated periodically as the ministry grows and evolves.

The leader of the dance ministry should schedule a meeting with the entire dance ministry and the SOP is reviewed line by line. At this meeting, questions can be answered and the foundational tone is set for guiding the ministry. It is a good standard of practice to have each member sign an agreement statement saying they read the SOP and will govern themselves according to the SOP document. This agreement statement can be kept in the church office and reviewed as necessary.

I know many of you are asking, "Why the need for a SOP, we are a church dance ministry." The intent of building a foundation for the ministry is set for all members in the SOP. The SOP serves as a consistent guide for the leader. Finally, the SOP can be updated, enhanced for greater accountability in the dance ministry. We all know that participating in any church ministry is strictly a volunteer position and participation in the dance ministry is no exception. However, there will be chaos in the dance ministry or any ministry where there are people from various backgrounds, levels of knowledge and spiritual connectedness. When I am working with dance ministries to establish an SOP, I always use the example of the workplace. When you are employed by any company or organization, you are given a human resources manual and in most cases you have some type of orientation. During that orientation, you are given detailed information about your place of employment; what time you need to arrive, what time you need to leave, information about vacation days, sick days and holidays. You are given information about insurance, the sexual harassment policy, personal development and the list continues as it relates to being successful in the workplace. We are expected to follow those rules and we sign paperwork stating that we will be in compliance to the rules of the organization. If we are not compliant, we can expect to be called into the supervisor's office, written up or even fired if we are unethical or our issues become out of hand.

If this is the standard in the workplace, why would we expect anything less in the kingdom of God? God is a God of excellence. We should be excellent in our service to Him. We have the standard operating procedure in place to make sure our dance ministries run as smoothly as things operate in the workplace. We will not offer God any less. There are procedures in place because things happen and we need to know in advance how to deal with the vicissitudes of life. As the leader of the ministry, when you can refer back to the SOP if an issue or conflict arises, you show that you are prepared and called to serve. When you go into the Pastor's office with guidelines for the ministry already in place, the Pastor will know that you are serious in your calling to lead the ministry and set the tone for excellence.

Many of you are asking what should be included in a dance ministry standard operating procedure document. I have included a sample for you to use as a guide. Use this sample draft as a tool to build your SOP for your dance ministry. Make it your own and revise it to suit your dance ministry. Having procedures in place will make a more efficient ministry and allow the spirit of God to use the ministry for its intended purpose and not to be a distraction.

SAMPLE DRAFT
Adult Dance Ministry Standard Operating Procedures
Called to the Kingdom Dance Ministry

The Called to the Kingdom (C2K) Dance Ministry is part of the Worship Arts Department at Your Church Name (YCN) and was developed to exalt God and support the vision of the Pastor. The dance ministry is responsible for bringing forth the message that reveals and communicates the Word of God through an outward expression of creative movements. Using the body as a temple of the Holy Spirit, and instruments of praise, the dance ministry aim is to glorify God through the creative expression of dance (Psalms 149:3; 150:4). The Ministry Standard Operating Procedures are designed to provide general direction, minimum requirements and dance ministers of Your Church Name (YCN).

a. **MEMBERSHIP**

a. Minimum age 18*.

Additional ages may be added at the discretion of the Dance Ministry Leader and the Worship Arts Director.

b. Have a teachable and learnable spirit. (Philippians 4:13)

c. Complete any church ministry prerequisite courses.

d. Personally accepted Jesus Christ as your Lord and Savior. (Romans 10:9-10)

e. Successfully complete YCN dance ministry training that includes a solo dance ministry presentation. (Some ministries have a three to six month dance ministry training period that must be completed before dancers can minister).

b. **REHEARSALS, TRAINING, MEETING AND ATTIRE**

Rehearsals:

a. Rehearsals are held Tuesday evening from 6:45 p.m. to 8:30 p.m. (list your rehearsal time here).

b. Dance ministers are expected to be on time for rehearsals. (Colossians 3:23; Philippians 2:3) Advance notification to Dance Ministry Leader is requested if you plan to be late or absent from rehearsal. Dance ministers that are consistently late may be asked to be non-participatory during rehearsals.

c. Rehearsal time changes will be communicated to dance ministers in advance.

d. A dance minister is ineligible to minister if they are absent from the rehearsal(s) immediately preceding a ministry presentation or do not attend 75% of the teaching.

e. A dance minister may not minister if they are late in arriving for Morning Prayer or rehearsal the morning of the presentation.

f. Dance ministers are requested to assist the ministry on dates that they are not ministering. (Romans 12:13)

g. Open enrollment for the dance ministry will be twice a year in October and April.

h. Dance ministers are required to learn what was missed if they are absent or late.

Meetings/Communication:

a. Active members of the Dance Ministry are encouraged to attend the monthly meetings that are scheduled for information, fellowship, and spiritual development.

Training:

a. All dancer ministers will be trained in praise, worship, and other styles of dance. Dance ministers will receive biblical dance teaching to include biblical foundations of dance, the tabernacles, the priesthood, garments, biblical colors, and characteristics of a dance minister, banners and flags, expressions of worship and dance ministry in the local church. (2 Tim 3:16-17)

Attire:

a. All dance ministers are responsible for the purchase and maintenance of their priestly ministry dance garments. Ministry garments must be neat, properly fitted, pressed and clean. Borrowing of garments is strongly discouraged. Dance ministers that do not have the proper garments will be ineligible to minister the presentation. (Romans 13:14)

b. Dance ministers should wear garments and shoes that allow free movement during rehearsal without being inappropriate. (Romans 13:14) Dance shoes are strongly encouraged.

c. No gum during rehearsal or ministry.

d. During ministry presentations, no jewelry other than wedding/ engagement rings, modest make-up (no stage make up), small stud earrings are permitted, and hair must be neat and pulled back from the face, long hair should be pinned up. Nail polish must be clear or neutral color.

Conduct and Conflict Resolution:
a. All dancers are expected to demonstrate Christ-like character and conduct at all times and strive to live a life consistent with the Word of God. (Ephesians 5:1-2)
b. Dancers are expected to regularly and consistently attend at least one of the weekly Sunday Worship services, and strongly encouraged to participate in Bible studies, Discipleship classes, and other sessions designed for spiritual growth and development. (Hebrews 10:25)
c. Dance ministers are required to tithe faithfully. (Malachi 3:10)
d. All matters of conflict or concern must be addressed between individuals; making every effort to keep the unity of the Spirit in the bond of peace. (Ephesians 4:3) Make every effort to keep the unity of the Spirit through the bond of peace. Should a conflict or concern arise within the Dance Ministry, every member will employ the resolution process outlined in Matthew 18:15-16.

Leave of Absence:
a. Dance ministers are requested to notify the Dance Ministry Leader if they will be on a leave of absence.
b. Dance ministers returning from an extended leave of absence may not minister in any service with the Dance Ministry until they have attended at least four (4) rehearsals/practices and have the proper attire.

Revision and Updates:
The ministry Standard Operating Procedures for the Dance Ministry may be updated periodically. No revisions will be distributed without the final approval of the Worship Arts Director and all revisions and updates will be disseminated to dancers in a timely manner.

This sample can be used to enhance your dance ministry. When there is no vision in place, the people perish. In this case, the dance ministry will perish. In most cases when people see there are no rules or guidelines in place and they can take advantage of the leader and come and go whenever they please, not show up until it is time to minister, you will have problems. When one group of people is judged by different standards than others, it will cause conflict in the ministry. **1 Corinthians 14:33** says [33] For God is not *the author* of confusion, but of peace, as in all churches of the saints. Confusion cannot exist in the ministry. I am reminded of one dance ministry that I worked with where the leader treated certain groups of dancers differently. After being in the ministry for months there were people that I heard were in the ministry but never attended a practice. On the day of ministry, yes that Sunday morning, they showed up and had on the garments and knew the dance but had never attended a practice. There were other people who missed the rehearsal before the Sunday ministry due to a child being ill and they could not minister, even though they knew the dance and had only missed the one rehearsal. When a new leader was selected and the SOP was put in place, dancers left the ministry because the standard had been established and God's order was put in place that did not include favoritism and mistreatment of certain people and the confusion ended and the ministry began to heal. God is not the author of confusion and a house divided will not stand. Ministers of dance, we need to bring stability and organization to our dance ministries. The vision cannot go forth if we maintain mess and not the message.

Dance Ministry Leader Responsibilities.
Dance ministry leaders must also be held accountable. Leadership is a major undertaking and should not be entered into lightly. Leaders are held at a higher standard than the members.

The dance ministry leader(s) should know the requirements of their duties and responsibilities. These duties and responsibilities should be written and discussed with the Pastor, Worship Arts directed or appointed liaison. Every person is accountable and the leader is no exception.

When there are ministries where there is more than one leader, duties and responsibilities can be divided based on the skill and technical capacities of each leader. It is always best to work in your area of strength and work to build your area of weakness as you lead by engaging in personal development. Stay in your lane, and don't let your pride get the best of you. If choreography is not your strength and you have never taken a dance class or attempted to choreograph a dance for a group, ask for assistance or yield to the leader or person in the dance ministry who has the experience. Remember you are held accountable; surround yourself with capable people who are called to assist you as you lead.

The duties listed below will give you an idea of how involved it is to lead a dance ministry. This will give you an idea of the responsibilities required. If you are the sole leader of the ministry, you may consider training someone in the ministry to assist you with certain tasks. If there are two or more leaders in the ministry, sit down and discuss your strengths and divide the responsibilities needed for your individual ministry. You may have other duties required by your church or ministry, so use this as a guide only to get you started as you set your foundation and establish order in the ministry.

Technical Teaching Leader Duties:
- Attend Your Church Name (YCN) Leadership meetings and trainings.
- Responsible for enforcing the ministry operating procedures.
- Be able to teach dance and dance techniques.
- Will teach biblical dance to include biblical foundations of dance, the tabernacles, the priesthood, garments, expressions of dance and worship, flags, banners and dance ministry in the local church.
- Be familiar with various styles of dance and facilitate all training of dance ministry members to include choreography workshops for current members.
- Choreograph routines for worship service and special events.
- Coordinate dance garment attire, banners and flags for dance ministry.
- Coordinates music with the Worship Arts director.

- Responsible for the scheduling outline of each rehearsal.
- Oversee the design and purchase process of garments and other needed props for the ministry and maintain dance vendor relationships.
- Responsible for the assistance of garments checks before each ministry presentation.
- Responsible for organizing dance ministry participation at dance conferences and hosting dance conferences.
- Will meet weekly with the Administrative leader and maintain a good working relationship and support for the advancement of the dance ministry.
- Act in the absence of the Administrative Leader.

Administrative Leader Duties:
- Attend (YCN) Leadership meetings and trainings.
- Responsible for enforcing the ministry operating procedures.
- Responsible for maintaining an accurate dance ministry attendance roster for each rehearsal and ministry event.

- Responsible for notifying the ministry of the rehearsal schedule and dance outreach ministry.
- Coordinate with facility manager about church use for rehearsals and any additional rehearsals and meetings.
- Responsible for disseminating videos and CDs to the dance ministry.
- Responsible for producing of videos, CDs, and overall music and technical equipment at each rehearsal.
- Responsible for working with (YCN) to coordinate ministry evangelism and outreach.
- Responsible for keeping an inventory of all dance ministry props and equipment.
- Coordinate use of props needed for each rehearsal.
- Responsible for coordinating Sunday morning ministry room for the ministry and any props needed for ministry.
- Responsible for the coordination of refreshments during times of worship.
- Responsible for handling the collection of special event fees due for the dance ministry and for notifying the ministry of member illness, death, birthdays, etc.

- Responsible for the assistance of garments checks before each ministry presentation.
- Responsible for garment alterations as needed.
- Will meet weekly with the Technical /Teaching leader and maintain a good working relationship and support for the advancement of the dance ministry.
- Act in the absence of the Technical/ Teaching Leader.

Dance ministry leadership is a considerable undertaking and involves a great deal of planning and responsibility. Leadership is a service unto God. Real leadership requires purpose over the position of being a leader. Your purpose or calling as the dance ministry leader is to proclaim Christ to others through the ministry of movement. Leadership is not who you lead, but how you lead. Lead on purpose. Lead in excellence, you are called to dance.

Chapter 9
Called to Leadership

Some people are just natural born leaders. I would like to put myself in that category. I was never really a follower. One of my first real leadership roles came at the end of my seventh grade year when I was asked to be the head majorette of my junior high school team. This was the first time that a rising ninth grader was not given the position, and yes there was a rising ninth grader on the team. This was my first time as a majorette in a formal school program; I had no previous leadership experience, only as a member of a competitive twirling team and dance team. I took my duties very seriously, and with a little assistance from my mother, I found a local seamstress to make our uniforms. I worked with her to design the uniforms and decided on the material and rhinestone design and application. I organized our team to attend majorette camp during the summer at an in state college for a week and put together our practice schedule and choreographed our routines. I loved taking the lead and was asked to serve in the positon my ninth grade year as well. I cannot think of a time in my life when I was not in a leadership capacity in some form or another. In college, I was the Coquette dance representative for two years and while in graduate school, the band director found me at a football game and asked me to be the graduate assistant for the team, which meant I was going to be paid for my leadership skills. Even as an adult, I was asked to take a leadership position in a dance ministry that I had only been a member of for a short period of time.

Leadership in dance ministry in my opinion is one of the hardest ministries to lead in the church. There are people in the dance ministry with different spiritual levels as well as skill levels and personalities. As the leader, you will need to have the competencies to manage all of those ministry levels in order to have an effective dance ministry. A dance leader has to be able to administrate in all of those areas without taking anything personally while keeping God at the center of the ministry. In the previous chapter there was a sample list of the duties and responsibilities for the leaders of a dance ministry, use the list as a guide to distribute responsibilities for the leaders in your dance ministry, there is always work for those who are called to dance.

In my opinion one of the best examples of leadership in the Bible is the story of Moses in Exodus, he was the leader of a nation of more than two million former slaves. He was surrounded by people constantly, but the people shared none of his vision or burdens. He had the concerns of the entire nation and the responsibility for their migration rested on him alone, as the people constantly reminded him whenever a difficulty arose. They had only been out of Egypt a few months, and he did not realize he would have to stand alone in this heavy burdened leadership role for four more decades. Then Moses received a visit from his father-in-law, Jethro in **Exodus 18: 13-23**. Jethro was worried about Moses and offered him some advice because he was concerned for Moses and the people. In verse 18, Jethro tells Moses, "You and these people who come to you will only wear yourselves out". What Moses experienced with the children of Israel, has nothing on what leaders are asked to administrate in dance ministries today.

The first piece advice was for Moses was he should restrict himself to what he alone could do, Jethro told him that he must be the people's representative before God and bring their disputes to him. He told Moses to teach them the decrees and laws, and show them the way to live and the duties they are to perform (versus 19-20). Moses work was twofold, he was to pray, he was to speak to God and to teach, and he was to make the decrees and laws of God known to the people.

The next advice was for Moses to appoint judges from the people. In **Exodus 18:21-23** Jethro advised Moses to appoint judges to all but the difficult judicial cases. He was to select capable men from all the people; men who fear God and are trustworthy. Select men who hate dishonest gain and appoint them as officials over thousands, hundreds, fifties and tens. Have them serve as judges for the people at all times, but have them bring every difficult case to you, the simple cases they can decide themselves. Leadership means delegation. We previously discussed in Chapter 8, responsibilities and duties for dance leaders. As dance ministry leaders, build up others around you to assist you in the work.

Jethro told Moses that following his advice would make his load lighter, because the selected people would share in the responsibilities with him. In verse 23, Moses learns that if he does this and God so commands, he will be able to stand the strain, and all these people will go home satisfied. Leaders, you need appointed people in your ministry to stand beside you to make your load lighter. You are a leader because:

- You have ability - the ability to hear cases impartially and to render wise judgment. **1 Peter 4:11.**
- You fear God - **Proverbs 9:10** declare that the fear of the Lord is the beginning of wisdom. Those who preside over the affairs of other human beings must have wisdom.
- You are reliable and trustworthy – you can be trusted, you are dependable. **Psalm 26:1.**
- You have integrity- you hate dishonest gain. Having integrity is important for those who were judges. God is calling dance ministry leaders who will render right judgement. **Psalm 26:1.**

Moses graciously accepted Jethro's advice in **Exodus 18:24-27**. Moses was not too proud to hear and accept an outside, objective opinion. Have you ever heard the saying "don't ask a question unless you have a solution"? Jethro, in the beginning of this story listened to all Moses had to say about what they had been through and Jethro praised God for all that He had done for Moses and the people. Jethro had a solution.

As leaders in dance ministry, there has to be a division of responsibility. If you are called to lead, know that in leadership:

- No one person in the church possesses all the necessary gifts to lead the ministry. God has given a wide distribution of people and gifts.
- No one person has the necessary time to do all that needs to be done.

Moses was a man of extraordinary ability, but even he could not do the work all by himself, at least not for long and Moses was the leader of millions people. If Moses could not do the work alone then neither can we do the work alone. We must look for others with whom you can share the work with. We must have others working alongside of us and in many cases allowing us to train them to do the work. Whether we are the leader, teacher or the student, we must be faithful, accountable and teachable as serving unto the Lord.

If you are the leader of your dance ministry, you were chosen because you are qualified for the job, both by your natural abilities and training by your spiritual qualities. We have to use our gifts wisely. Just like your Pastor cannot do the work of the ministry alone, dance ministry leaders have to be mature and focus on what we can do best and on what we have to offer. One sad result of trying to do it all ourselves is that we overlook the talents of others, robbing them of the opportunity to serve God.

When we are called as leaders or pursuing leadership in ministry it is because have the ability, we are capable, we fear God, we are trustworthy, and we have integrity. Keep in mind the following:

- Do not be distracted.
- A wise leader can not only give good advice but also receive it.
- Always have a teachable spirit.
- Right relationships are important, always build good relationships with people.
- Guard your daily time with the Lord.
- Don't get busier, get smarter. Simplify your life.
- Delegate in the dance ministry and in your home life.
- You can say no to the distractions but say yes to what God has for you. There is always time to do what God wants you to do.

Chapter 10
Called to Technique

Technique as defined by Merriam-Webster is the way that a person performs basic physical movements or skills or a way of doing something by using special knowledge or skill. God is a God of order. In mastering any skill, it is God's desire that we study and polish that talent, developing it to its maximum effect to the glory, honor, and power of God (Stevenson, 1998).

I have heard the question asked endless times over the years, who is the more anointed dancer, someone who has a technical background in dance such as ballet, modern or jazz or someone who has never taken any classes but has a God given gift for dance. Let me say this, I have seen trained dancers in the church, I am talking about dancers who started taking dance lessons at age five and they know turnout, they know tendu, arabesque, port de bras, rond de jambe and they can flip, spin, turn, leap, kick and split like no one else, but this background and knowledge does not make that dancer more anointed. I know dancers who have never taken a dance lesson in their life but minister some of the most powerful and anointed dances I have ever seen.

Whether you are a formally trained dancer or not, there has to be some level of technique executed in your dance movement in order for you to communicate a clear message. Technique is the basis of all fundamentals of dance, from holding your body correctly while dancing, to executing skills properly in dance ministry. Solid, foundational technique extends across all areas of dance, and Christian dance is no exception. Becoming skillful is pleasing to God (Stevenson, 1998).

Ballet is foundational and can be used as a point of reference when teaching technique in dance ministry. When teaching ballet in connection to liturgical dance ministry, I always tell ministers of dance that I am not trying to make them "ballerinas", but that ballet is used as a foundational tool to assist in the clear communication of ministry and as a tool to expand their dance vocabulary. I then start teaching the ballet positions and basic movements, asking each dancer to work at their level of comfort. Technique for me includes your posture when you are dancing. Yes, we all have different skill sets, but a pointed toe when the foot leaves the ground speaks excellence during ministry. Basic open arm movements with straight arms offer an excellent praise. Technique requires practice and it is God's desire that we minister to the people on His behalf in excellence.

As we build a solid foundation, choreography is a step to incorporate technique skills to the minister in dance. Choreography is the art of building dances. To begin, organize your thoughts and materials and most importantly, pray. A few basic points to remember as you choreograph dances include:

- A dance must enhance and embellish worship and praise and not cause confusion. God is not the author of confusion. (I Corinthians 14:33)
- Your message must be a clearly communicated message that flows, is fluent and is communicated throughout the entire length of the song.
- The movements are like words, you put the words together to make sentences and the sentences form phrases and the phrases form paragraphs.
- In the end, you have an entire essay. You have a complete dance that connects and is clearly communicated.

When listening to music and developing movement, remember the following terms:

Phrase: a sequence of movements that is commonly four to eight measures long, the simplest unit of a dance form. Phrases build upon one another in an organized progression so that again one feels a sense of beginning, middle and end or continuity.

Sequence: a series of movements that is longer than a phrase, for example, two or three phrases together; a combination. Combinations can be repeated during the dance and changed if the dance is repetitive.

Transition: a bridge from one phrase of movement into the next; should fit with the other movement and not be noticeable.

Continuity: this is unity, the natural flowing of one phrase into another in an organized progression giving a sense of a beginning, middle and end.

Choreographic or Compositional Devices
Directions:
An important part of choreography is being able to connect and minister directly with your intended audience. Using directional facings add clarity as you build clarity in the movements for your dance ministry. Direction is simply the way that you are facing. There are eight directional faces; starting to your front with one, rotating clockwise to the diagonal is two, the side to your right is three, the back right diagonal is four, the back is five, the diagonal back is six, the side is seven and the front diagonal is eight. Your strongest facing is forward. It is always good to have a variety of facings in your choreography but motivation for movement should just not be to fill space.

Levels:
There are different physical levels to consider in choreography. When you incorporate different levels, there is more freedom to clearly communicate your message and the intended audience is engaged in the movement. Levels should be included based on the skill and physical limitations of the dancers. The levels below have been compiled from The Eagles Network (TEN) modules.

- Level 1 – **Humility** – Laying prostrate, face to the ground. Arms can be above the head or out to the side. (Proverbs 15:33)
- Level 2 – **Submission** – Sitting back on the heels. (Proverbs 3:5)
- Level 3 – **Surrender** – Lifted up on knees, pressing through the hips. Body in L formation. (Psalm 37:5)
- Level 4 – **Yield** – A deep plie, bend of one or both knees, lunges. (Jeremiah 29:11)
- Level 5 - **Restoration** – To stand straight up, feet flat on the ground. (Psalm 51:12)
- Level 6 – **Seek** – Releve, rise up on your toes. (Matthew 6:33)
- Level 7 – **Rejoice** – Jump with one or both feet off the ground. (Philippians 4:4)
- Level 8 – **Ascension** – Standing on top a pew, chair, pulpit, alter, people. (Psalm 24:3-4)

Please note that the information given on directional facing and levels are choreography enhancements. Remember we are communicating a clear message as ministers of dance. Pray and ask God to give you movement or seek the assistance of other skilled ministers as needed. I remember when I first started out in ministry, I connected with many dancers in my area through workshops and dance worship services. I mentioned to one dancer that I was asked to minister at a women's meeting and I was having difficulty with choreography and music and in no time at all we were meeting and listening to music and working on movement.

The Marriage: Music and Choreography

Music is an important part in choreography. Just as a choreographer uses movement tell a story. Music allows you to marry the words and the movement. Based on the style of song and lyrics, you transfer your vision of a dance into movement. When you begin to listen to songs for dance ministry, pray and ask God to select a song appropriate to the theme (if there is one), the dance ministry and the audience.

Guidelines to follow:

- Identify your audience and the purpose of the choreography. Start exploring songs that will connect them to your choreography. Avoid selecting songs that have recently been over-played on radio and in the media. You want a song that will stand out and be as original as your movement. You want the audience to connect with the song, so you probably want to stay away from anything too abstract.

- The music must connect to the dancers. Consider the age range of the dancers and the types of movements that could connect and be universal for all members.
- Consider the emotion and feeling you want to communicate. Just be sure the lyrics and melody of the song do not contradict the emotion of the movements in your choreography.
- Once you select a song for ministry, find appropriate scriptures that coincide with the ministry piece. You can also involve your dance ministry, ask them to locate scriptures that reflect the heart of the song.
- Length of music and repetition: Some dances may take longer to teach than others. When choreographing, take into account how much time you have to teach the dance. This can help you determine the length for your dance. If you have only a few practices to teach and minister a dance, maybe incorporate only a few formation

changes and keep the movements simple or less intricate. Consider adding technical skills in which your team has already mastered. Choose a style that your team picks up quickly and that they are most comfortable learning.

Technical skill and the anointing work hand in hand to create life changing dance ministry. Allow the Lord to use you as His vessel to minister on His behalf. I am reminded of **Acts 17:28**, For in Him we live and move and have our being. You are **Called to Dance**, allow the Lord to make you technique ready and move in excellence.

Chapter 11
Walk Worthy of Your Calling

Dance ministry is a lifestyle. When we walk worthy of our calling, we effect change in the kingdom of God. That is why I am so attached to **Ephesians 4:1**, I want to live a life worthy of the calling that I have received. If I am not walking worthy, then my calling is in vain. I mentioned previously how I would sit in church when I was a little girl and see myself dancing. My parents worked hard and spent money for me to train and develop my gift while growing up. As an adult God has allowed me to redefine how He would like to use my previously acquired skills. Shame on me not to use the calling that I have received in some way to glorify God, especially when dancing in the church was what I envisioned as a child.

Everyone is not called to dance ministry. This statement is true for the formally trained dancer and those who are not trained. Walking worthy of the calling of dance is a lifestyle. I have had people come up to me and say they wanted to be in dance ministry because they did not want to see me dancing by myself. I questioned their commitment but was obedient in starting biblical background and training with them, each time when we discussed lifestyle within a matter of weeks, no days they told me that they would not be able to complete the training. Let's be clear, I am not perfect and I fall short of the glory of God all the time, but when He calls you to a dance, He will make sure you are walking worthy. Over the years there has been test after test after test, I have failed some of them. I have missed out on opportunities out of fear and lack of finances, but even during the lean years, He never allowed me to sit on my calling.

When I teach lifestyle, I like to use the visual of being dissected. It is what is on the inside of us that comes out when we minister. When we talk about what we look like on the inside, there should also be a standard of what flows to the outside. That standard is our lifestyle. If I am teaching lifestyle and foundation, what does my heart look like, what about my hands? I am reminded of **Matthew 12:34,** for out of the abundance of the heart the mouth speaketh.

If we look at our anatomy as dancers, what would we find? Another word for anatomy is composition or make up. In order to present our bodies as a living sacrifice, our lifestyle must be composed or made up of the right material. We should have the attitude of a humble servant and the only objective is to glorify God. We must consecrate ourselves in the word from head to toe. Walking worthy of the call to dance requires a relationship. It requires time spent alone with God in the Word, in prayer and in meditation.

As we walk worthy of our calling, let's meditate and study the scriptures below and allow the Holy Spirit to reveal areas of our lives that we need to cultivate as we are called to be more effective as ministers of dance.

- Our mind, thoughts and focus should be on God.

  Head – Leviticus 8:12 - Then he poured some of the anointing oil on Aaron's head and anointed him, to consecrate him.

- We should use our hands to build others up in inspiration and by a touch of correction in love.

  Hands – Psalm 63:4 - So I will bless You as long as I live; I will lift up my hands in Your name.

- Our arms should reflect the beauty, comfort and safety of Gods arms.

  Arms – Psalm 136:12 - With a strong hand, and with a stretched out arm: for his mercy *endureth* forever.

- Our shoulders carry the message of the good news.

  Shoulders - Luke 15:5 - When he has found it, he lays it on his shoulders, rejoicing.

- Our mouth is for positive praise. May our words be acceptable in His sight.

Mouth – Psalm 19:14 - Let the words of my mouth, and the meditation of my heart, be acceptable in thy sight, O LORD, my strength, and my redeemer.

- Our hearts should be guarded, it is the wellspring of life and we should seek transformation in spirit and in truth - **Proverbs 4:23**.
  Heart - Psalm 26: 2 - Examine me, O LORD, and prove me; try my reins and my heart.
- Our knees allow is to assume a posture of prayer.
  Knees – Ephesians 3: 14 - For this cause I bow my knees unto the Father of our Lord Jesus Christ.
- Our feet are used to deliver the message of the Great Commission.
  Feet – Romans 10: 15 - And how shall they preach, except they be sent? As it is written, how beautiful are the feet of them that preach the gospel of peace, and bring glad tidings of good things!
- Our body is a living sacrifice used for God's glory and His righteousness.
  Body – Romans 12:1 - Therefore, I urge you, brothers, in view of God's mercy, to offer your bodies as living sacrifices, holy and pleasing to God--this is your spiritual act of

worship. **Romans 12:1 (AMP)** I APPEAL to you therefore, brethren, *and* beg of you in view of [all] the mercies of God, to make a decisive dedication of your bodies [presenting all your members and faculties] as a living sacrifice, holy (devoted, consecrated) and well pleasing to God, which is your reasonable (rational, intelligent) service *and* spiritual worship.

Walking worthy in dance ministry requires that we build our foundation on Jesus Christ, study the Word, and have a lifestyle that represents Christ. If you are called to dance, you should know is that dance ministry has nothing to do with dance, it's all about worship. Being called to dance is about a relationship with Christ. Dance ministry is Christ focused and not self-focused. What I have learned over the years is that each of us has a different experience how we are called, but the common thread in the calling is hearing the voice of God and moving in obedience to the call.

The intent in building a foundation is for dance in the church to be restored as a worship gift from God. Although godly dance has suffered violent assault and at one point almost completely vanished, Satan's original plan to completely steal dance away from the church has entirely failed

(Stevenson, 1998). If you have accepted the call to dance, know that the Prophet Jeremiah declared in **Jeremiah 31:13**; young women will dance and be glad, young men and old as well. I will turn their mourning into gladness; I will give them comfort and joy instead of sorrow. You are a part of the prophetic call to restore dance; restoration begins with our total surrender and obedience to God. Building the foundation necessary to our calling to dance is imperative. You are **Called to Dance**; walk worthy of the calling you have received in Christ Jesus.

References

Cornwall, J. (1998). The Philosophy of Worship: Exploring the Components of Worship. Christian Life Publications.

Daniels, M. (1981). The Dance in Christianity: A History of Religious Dance Through the Ages. New York: Paulist Press.

Easton, M. G. (2005). Illustrated Bible Dictionary. New York: Cosimo Classics.

Eyeman, Juliette. The Significance of Dance: Why Satan Is Dancing While the Church Drags It's Feet.

Gagne, R., Kane, T., and Ver Eeck, R. (1984). Dance in Christian Worship. Washington: Pastoral

Israel & New Breed: Alive in South Africa (2010). Integrity Music

Kovacs, A. (1996). Dancing into the Anointing. Shippensburg, PA: Treasure House.

Leonard, R.C. (1997). Worship in the Early Church. www.laudemont.org.

Levy, D. (2013). The Tabernacle: Shadows of the Messiah. The Friends of Israel Gospel Ministry, Inc.

Levy, David M. (1993) The Tabernacle : Shadows of the Messiah (Its Sacrifices, Services, and Priesthood ; See How the Tabernacle Relates to Jesus). Friends of Israel Gospel Ministry.

Matthew Henry's Commentary on the Whole Bible: Complete and Unabridged by Henry. Matthew (2008) Hardcover. Hendrickson Publishers.

McGee, J. V. (1984). Genesis through Revelation. Thomas Nelson.

Merriam-Webster. (2004). The Merriam-Webster Dictionary (Revised edition). Springfield, Mass: Merriam-Webster Mass Market.

Mettinger, T. (2005). In Search of God: The Meaning and Message of the Everlasting Names. (F. H. Cryer, Trans.). Philadelphia: Augsburg Fortress Publishers.

Orr, J. (1939). The International Standard Bible Encyclopedia, 5 volume set. Wm B. Eerdmans Pub. Co.

Pickett, Fuscia (2000). Worship Him: Discover The Joy of Pure Spiritual Worship (First Edition edition). Lake Mary, Florida: Charisma House.

Publishers, H. B. (1991). Holman Bible Dictionary. Nashville, Tenn: Broadman & Holman Publishers.

Richards, J. B. (2001). Grace: The Power To Change. New Kensington, PA: Whitaker House.

Stevens, R. P. (1997). The Complete Book of Everyday Christianity: An A-To-Z Guide to Following Christ in Every Aspect of Life. (R. J. Banks, Ed.). Intervarsity Publishing.

Stevenson, A. (1998). Restoring the Dance: Seeking God's Order. Shippensburg, PA: Treasure House.

Strong, J. (2010). The New Strong's Expanded Exhaustive Concordance of the Bible (Expanded edition). Thomas Nelson.

Tuppim, Qan (2003). Biblical Accounts of Belly Dance in the Ancient New East, Part II. www.GildedSerpent.com.

Vine, W. E., and Unger, M. (1996). Vine's Complete Expository Dictionary of Old and New Testament Words: With Topical Index. Nashville: Thomas Nelson.

Zondervan. (2011). Holy Bible. Zondervan.

About the About the Author

Paryn Wallace discovered her calling for dance at an early age and is honored to be able to use her gift for the Kingdom of God. Starting out at an early age, Paryn has been involved in dance and has taken dance classes and has been a teacher of ballet, tap, jazz and baton twirling. Paryn is a 2007 Eagle International Training Institute (EITI) graduate and Golden Eagle recipient under the mentorship of Apostle Pamela Hardy. Paryn also graduated from EITI School of Intercessory in 2010, the EITI School of the Prophetic in 2010 and EIAI Eagles International Authors Institute in 2015.

Paryn has been involved in many facets of ministry over the years to include serving as the Women's Ministry Leader, Dance Ministry Leader, Fisher of Men Administrator and Special Event Assistant with several ministries in South Carolina, Georgia and New Jersey. She served as a Minister and Pastor under the training of Dr. Charles A. Wallace II, founder and Pastor of Hebron World Church in Georgia.

Received through a vision after graduating from EITI, Paryn is the founder and teacher of *"Called to the Kingdom Dance Ministries"* (*Ephesians 4:1*). Through Called to the Kingdom, Paryn has taught weekly dance lessons in ballet, liturgical dance and sign language to children and adults in her local community and surrounding area.

Paryn has been a teacher with The Eagles Network (TEN) since its inception. She was a member of an evangelist outreach dance ministry in Georgia and served as a Georgia TEN teacher before relocating to New Jersey. Currently, she is the New Jersey State Leader for EITI, and teaches for New Jersey TEN North and New Jersey TEN South/Philadelphia. She is a member of the National Liturgical Network and AME Liturgical Dance Commission under the mentorship of Rev. Eyesha Marable. Paryn travels to teach Biblical Foundations of Dance, The Priesthood and Garments, Moses Leadership Style, Standard Operating Procedures, Goal Setting, Seeing Beyond, and Leaders Empowered to Change their Lives for several dance ministries throughout the United States.

Paryn is married to Pastor and Psalmist Dr. Charles Wallace II, the founder of Hebron World Church in Georgia. Pastor Charles has served as an executive pastor and psalmist for numerous ministries. Charles and Paryn are the parents of three sons; Charles III, Carson and Caedan. Her desire is to see dance and the arts restored back to its rightful creator and originator, God.

For additional information about

Paryn Wallace
And
Called to the Kingdom Dance Ministries
Or to arrange dance ministry workshops, conferences,
And leadership teaching seminars
Contact:

Email: paryn@areyoucalled.org
Telephone: 1-844-885-5664
Fax: 609-228-4880

Website: www.areyoucalled.org

Called to the Kingdom Dance Ministries

Paryn Wallace
paryn@areyoucalled.org
1-844-885-5664

Paryn Wallace –
Founder and Instructor

Eagles International Training
Institute
2007 Eagle of the Year Graduate

- Consultation for dance ministries and leaders
- Workshops, Conferences and Special Events
- Biblical Foundations of Liturgical Dance
- Priesthood & Garments
- Leadership for Dance Ministers
- Ministry Standard Operating Procedures
- Goal Setting
- Seeing Beyond – Goal Setting Part 2
- Leaders Empowered to Change their Lives

www.ingramcontent.com/pod-product-compliance
Lightning Source LLC
LaVergne TN
LVHW051246080426
835513LV00016B/1759